Intimacy Today

His heart...My heart

Intimacy Today: His Heart – My Heart
ISBN: #978-1-60920-041-1
©2012 Nellie LaBouef

Printed in the United States of America

Library of Congress Cataloging-in-Publication Data

API
Ajoyin Publishing, Inc.
P.O. 342
Three Rivers, MI 49093
www.ajoyin.com

The author's use of commas and capital letters for emphasis is intentional and based on poetic license.

Please direct your inquiries to admin@ajoyin.com

I am sure the Lord and the angels were standing on the balcony of heaven on June 14, 1957, and with a tender breath of air, He blew into those tiny little lungs. With a gentle smile, God and the angels saw those beautiful, big brown eyes open for the first time, and the Lord said, "Watch out world, here she comes!"

Your steadfast service for our Lord is amazing and an inspiration for me and countless others who are touched by your life. Since we met in late 1972, wow, and now with three children, wow, what an adventure! I am truly a blessed man. (Love you the most!)

Thank you, Lord, (and Nellie),

—Mark A. LaBouef, (Nellie's husband)

Mom, I think it is great! I do not read it daily, but it seems the times that I do read it, that seems to be the days where I need it most, and it never fails to speak to me. I love you, Mom, you really do have a heart of gold in a world that seems to just not care very much, and I will always respect that of you!

—Mark LaBouef Jr. (Nellie's Firstborn Son)

May God bless this book and use it for his glory. It never ceases to amaze me how the Lord has used your life. I look back to when we were kids and see my little sister and say, Praise God, she has been called to His work. You are doing it, and have grown to be quite a special woman. I admire and respect you.

—Love, your big brother Bob (Nellie's Brother)

"To my sisters and brothers in Christ, I believe that Nellie has truly found the "intimacy" that we all desire with our Lord and Savior. May these daily conversations and prayers grow you in your walk with our Jesus. May these words be a tool to bring you further as you journey closer to Him.

—In His love, Georgia Robinson" (Nellie's Cousin)

I'm so excited Aunt Nellie! I had no idea you were doing a book! Praise the LORD! I think a book format would be such a great thing because although I love reading the daily email, I also love getting comfy in a corner somewhere with my Bible, and a good devotional book to guide me along and to have the place (lines at the bottom) to write my own response from my heart would be AWESOME! I think it's a fabulous idea. I would buy bunches of them to give to my friends so they would be blessed too! THANK YOU, for all of the hard work you've done thus far for this project, and for furthering the Kingdom! I love you!

—Christina Johnson, (Nellie's Niece)

I've known Nellie from the time she was a young bride, new to our family, and a young Christian, new to the family of God.

"Niece Nellie," as we call her, has matured in her roles as wife, mother and grand-mother. At the same time she grew in her relationship to the Lord she loves. In her book, Nellie shares from the intimacy of that relationship—her intimate conversations with a living God. By sharing, Nellie hopes her readers will come to know that intimacy, too.

—*"Aunt Jan" Wise, author of the Bible study, Free From Worry*

It is a refreshing to actually read of one's interaction with a holy God! Nellie has shared with us some insights into how God deals with His children and how we respond to His grace and love. I highly commend this reading to you believing that it will encourage your faith and compel you to engage with the Father.

—*Randy Howard, Senior Leader of the Gate (Nellie's Pastor)*

Nellie's article series, *Intimacy* includes biblical scriptures expressed in contemporary language, giving, and assisting Christians to excel in their God-given purpose. *Intimacy* has received outstanding reviews from readers and colleagues who have commented positively with regards to achieving their personal triumphs as they read and experience the profound narratives.

Desert Rose Magazine thanks God for Nellie LaBouef, as she uses her gifts as a conduit for spiritual freedom for many souls!

—*Barbara James*

I must say the messages I have received from you mean so much. You send me the word of God and no matter where I am I read them. I could be having a bad day and the words you send me just remind me that Jesus loves me no matter what. I could be doing something I shouldn't, and the word of God sets me straight. I'm so thankful for your messages, they lift me up. I feel the intimacy with every word. The idea of a book is beyond questioning or doubt. I endorse this wonderful idea and wish you much success ...

—*Mario*

I was just looking at some of your devotionals and I got so blessed. Thank you so much. This devotional has added to that perfect peace I need that the Lord promises His people. Again, THANK YOU!

—*Nancy Apodaca*

Intimacy Today is a Holy Spirit anointed, "rhema" word imparting breath of life to those who choose to read and engage with the process of a deep intimate conversation with their Lord and the Lover of their souls. There is a buyer beware caution here. Once this purchase is made and you invest in intimacy with God, your heart will no longer be your own but a shared vessel of love through which God's unconditional love is dispensed to the people in your world.

—*Hellen Meade*

After reading the selected scriptures and then Nellie's writings, it's as if time stands still and you are alone with Father God. The world disappears and He is loving you, encouraging you, and at times disciplining you. A warmth fills you, you rejoice to go on with your day.

—*Joyce Bouchard*

I read your *Intimacy* every day and marvel at your walk with our Lord. Your Joy and love of the word inspires me to try to connect in my own way as you have done. I will pray that this book will inspire anyone and everyone who gets to enjoy it. God bless you for your courage and dedication. I admire you.

—*Shirley Cleveland*

How exciting for you...I always love reading your daily prayers...as I am growing closer in intimacy with the Lord.

—*Jane Blakewell*

God has used these daily devotions to comfort me, encourage me, and confirm His word to me. I look forward every day to what the Lord is saying and your response through the Holy Spirit. I know these conversations take place during the third watch (3:00 a.m. to 6:00 a.m.) and it is such a testimony of how we can seek Him early in the morning and how He hears us and answer us and desires that incredible two-way intimacy. Nellie, I want to share with you what the Lord put on my heart regarding your book. He was showing me how powerful this will be for those who know they are supposed to have intimacy with Him but don't know what that intimacy looks like. They say a picture is worth a 1,000 words. Your book will be a picture of intimacy and a road map as to how to experience it. I am so excited about the lives it will touch and change and UPGRADE their relationships with the Lord.

—*Cheryl Halseth*

It's a true blessing, every morning when I come into work, (I do not have a computer at home) I can't wait to see what the Lord has to say to me. His words make the day go better and remind me to pray for things I may have forgotten.

—Joyce Depezenski

It is such a blessing to read these personal words from and to God. I am sometimes amazed at the timing and application for my own life. Only God knows what I need each day and He's chosen to speak through this vessel to accomplish much encouragement, much conviction, much hope, much endurance.

—Lynne Behrns

I feel the Lord is speaking directly to me when I read your daily devotions and the intimate prayer that follows is straight from my heart. The Holy Spirit is woven into every word.

—Kathy Renfro

As I ponder the writings of your book, I have found *Intimacy Today* to bring such a profound awakening! It's an incredible process of finding our way to interact with God on an individual basis. This isn't just an inspirational way to start the day, it IS a journey to the truth of God for us. This book brings its reader into an amazing— beyond limits—interaction with God. What a Gift. Thank You and God Bless You.

—Glory Bayer

Words are not enough to explain the amount of blessing this ministry has been for me. In my life, using this as a daily devotional, the Lord has met me right where I am. From getting my prayer life together, to calling me to account, the Lord has reached me in love and truth. Many times ... I have found peace here.

—Lucy Walker

I look forward to receiving *Intimacy Today!* I take it seriously, that the Lord is speaking to me, keeping me on the right track, meeting my needs for the day, giving me clear direction, soothing my hurts and reassuring me that He is near me. It causes me to get my focus back on Him when I stray, (but of course I never do that)! Conviction is good for my soul, and gives me hope for tomorrow.

—Tamara Ricci

Intimacy is very special to me, I look forward to receiving the devotions each morning. Although I may not get to read them each day I have saved each one in it's own, "Nellie's file." Each intimate conversation is so in-tune with the words of our Father, which makes it special when the Holy Spirit converses back to the Father. It absolutely wows me! Thank you Nellie for sharing this open door of intimacy that our Father has for all who will enter!

—*Deborah Harris*

Ever have one of those days when you just can't get motivated to have your quiet time with the Lord? At times, all of us need a little push, a gentle reminder of how truly blessed we are to belong to the King of Kings. That's what *Intimacy* is all about—looking at what the Word of God says to us and responding from our hearts. Nellie has walked through difficult days, as well as those filled with happiness. Along the way, she has developed an intimate, conversational relationship with the Father. She invites you to come along as she walks with Jesus.

—*Ruth Justis*

These inspirational messages are wonderful. I'm glad they're being put into a book. I print the email messages and put them in a notebook, as when I'm at the computer, I don't seem to take the time to let the wonderful words seep into my spirit.

—*Dorothy Inglese*

Intimacy Today, written by Nellie, has a way of bringing God's Word alive. Reading them is like receiving fresh manna from heaven. It reminds me of the scripture in Exodus 16 that talks about how God gave the Israelites fresh manna from Heaven daily that tasted like honey wafers. His blessings are new every morning. I look forward to reading every day a love letter from my Heavenly Father and then dwelling on the in-depth response back to Him; sweet like a honey wafer Thanks, Nellie for blessing us with your wonderful gift of writing.

—*Jamie Holland*

You will be totally blessed by this book! Nellie has a way of exuding joy as she shares her intimate conversations with God. As her heart, through the Holy Spirit, communicates to your soul, you will undoubtedly move closer to Him and come to know His love for you in a deeper way than you ever imagined! As you "listen" with your spiritual ears, there's room to write it all down, too! God has blessed Nellie with the capacity to bring others closer to Him. I love this book.

—*Lynn Courtney*

Intimate conversations have blessed me on so many levels, as I know it will others. The richness of His Word fills my spirit every time I read them. As I'm being refreshed, it awakens the emotions of my soul, which sends His delight through my being, prompting my body to respond. Extra pages can serve as a journal of your own journey into intimate conversations with the Lord.

—*Johanna Sharp*

Dear Ones
Each day as I check my emails, I am blessed to receive The Word from my very dear friend and sister in Christ, Nellie. Most of time, things in my life are fine and full of excitement for what the day will bring, but there are the days when this is not the case. At those times, my God comes in and delivers just the right words through Nellie's writings. As I continue to read His word each Day, I know that I am loved and cared for. God has a way of showing up, no matter the circumstances. Be blessed in knowing You Are Loved with the greatest love of all, from our Father in Heaven, Jesus.

—*Christine Bumpus*
President, Aglow Ridgecrest, CA.

Just wanted to let you know that one of the new ladies who is receiving your Intimacy daily told me today that she is SO blessed by your writings She absolutely loves receiving them every day, and she really looks forward to it. Thanks for taking the time to touch each one of us in a special way each day with this beautiful and meaningful devotion :)

—*Melissa Mongeaus*

I am so grateful for the daily devotion you share with me and so many others. Thank you! It's devotions like these that inspire my heart to sing and create and release what the Lord has put within me. Nellie, you are a unique and powerful woman of God. Your love for Him is evident in the many lives that He touches through you. Keep it up; keep flowing!

—*Brother Mike Garcia*

Thank you. You were praying exactly what was in my heart this morning! It lines up with my own prayer.

—*Ingrid Bruce*

Intimacy Today

His heart...My heart

Nellie LaBouef

Foreword

SOME TIME AGO NOW, as the Lord began to call me closer to Himself, He asked me to begin to study the heart of David, and I did!

A year or so later, He began to tell me to have a heart like David's, and before I knew it, I realized, I did!

Some time later, Sherry, a friend of mine gave me a devotional as a gift. It was one I couldn't put down, unlike the many others I had owned. It was very much in tune with this new heart God had begun to draw out of me. God used this, and many things to draw me deeper in, closer to Him than I had ever experienced.

Then one day He asked me to begin an Intimate and Conversational Relationship with Him. I responded to Him, "But Lord, I Pray!" And He said,

"Yes, but prayer is a petitioning, this is more! Intimacy and communion like never before!" And He was right; like never before it is!

Now you too can read it! He has had me put some of these Intimate conversations into Words in this book for you! Never be concerned or ashamed if you have not experienced this Intimacy, Yet!

I've known Him for many years, and yet I've learned deeper things, as I've followed His lead, watching and listening throughout the day. He always has something to say in every circumstance of your life, continually.

Let all else go, and find a Quiet place, just sit in Silence, turn everything off, and simply Read, and Enjoy, then Listen, He has Dreams on His Heart to share with only You, moment by moment!

Then after you've read and heard His Gentle Whispers in your heart, write them down and you'll find that they are led by the Spirit, they don't even sound like you, and you are ministered to by them.

Intimacy! This is where you learn to know Him, More Abundantly! Your Great Reward! Bridegroom! The Coming One, to whom you're Engaged! Get to Know Him, Now! Be comfortably ready for Face to face!

"Read slowly and enjoy!"

— Nellie

Ephesians 5:20; Psalm 118:1; Psalm 89:14–15

～

My Child, give thanks to Me always, in the Name of my Son, Jesus. Give thanks to Me for I Am Good! My Faithful Love endures forever. Righteousness and justice are the foundation of My throne. My unfailing Love and Truth walk before you as attendants. Happy are those who hear My Joy-filled call to worship, for they will walk in the Light of My Presence.

FATHER, my heart is full of thankfulness for You and for Your Presence. My mind is filled with thoughts of You. As I proceed into this very day, may the Light and Love of Your Presence be evident in me and an attraction to those you place in my path. Obedience is my goal, every day of my life. Here I am Lord, "send me" ... In Jesus' Name, Amen!

I Thessalonians 5:16–18; James 4:7–8; Romans 15:13

~

Be joyful always! Never stop conversing with Me intimately. Be thankful in all circumstances, for this is My will for you, as you belong to My Son, Jesus. Resist the devil, and he will flee from you. Come close to Me, and I will come close to you. Wash your hands of sin, and purify your heart, for your loyalty is divided between Me and the world. I, your God, am your source of hope. I will fill you completely with Joy and Peace because you trust Me. You will overflow with confident hope through the Power of My Holy Spirit.

FATHER, I choose to practice thanking you in all things, <u>really</u>. Let me begin today! I ask you by your Holy Spirit and Power to intervene in my thoughts and prompt me moment by moment so that I'll be successful. I want an intimate conversational relationship with You, like I have not yet known. Thank You for the gradual change I already feel. I look forward to the amazing days ahead with a closer walk with You. With You, I Can Do ALL Things! In Jesus Name, Amen!

Psalm 118:23–24; Psalm 116:16–18

It is all My doing, and it's wonderful to see. This is the day I've made, rejoice and be glad in it! Oh My servant, yes, you are My servant born into My household, I've freed you from chains. Offer Me the sacrifice of thanksgiving, and call on My Name, for I Am your Lord!

FATHER, I thank you that you have already planned my day. I can walk into it fully aware of that fact. Now all I have to do is my part, "stay focused" on You! I will be thankful for all things, and I'll be blessed to Be a blessing throughout this day, to You first and to anyone You choose. I'll watch for you in the beauty of the day, and walk closer to you in any darkness that comes my way. I know You're with me and that causes me to rejoice. In Jesus' Name, Amen!

Colossians 3:15; Acts 9:16; Revelation 19:3–6

~

Let the Peace that comes through knowing Jesus, My Son, rule in your heart. As a member of the one Body, you are called to live in Peace, and to always be thankful. I will show you how much you must suffer for My Name's sake. Praise your Lord! Though the smoke ascends from that city forever and ever. Praise Me, all you servants and all who fear Me from the least to the greatest. Praise Me, for I Am the Lord your God Almighty who reigns.

FATHER, my desire is that praise and thankfulness unto You would be the very fiber of who I am as my heart is to please You and hear Your voice at all times. I "relinquish all control to You," with a knowing that only then will my heart truly overflow with praise and thankfulness along with heaven's "Hallelujahs." I love You Lord! In Jesus' Name, Amen!

I Peter 5:7; Ephesians 3:16–19

My Child, give Me all your concerns and cares, for I care for you.

From My glorious unlimited resources I will empower you with inner strength through My Spirit. Then Jesus, who makes His home in your heart, as you trust Him, will cause your roots to grow deep into My Love and keep you strong. You'll have My power to understand as all My children should, how wide, how long, how high, and how deep My Love is. You'll experience the Love of Jesus, though it is too Great to understand fully. Then you'll be made complete with all the fullness of Life and power that comes from Me.

FATHER, I choose to spend more time focusing on the many facets of Your Love for Me. I will quiet myself and think on the things that are gifts from You, and be thankful for them. I Love You Lord, and I lift my voice to praise and worship You, my Savior, this very day! With all of my heart, I pray. In Jesus' Name, Amen!

Isaiah 58:11; Isaiah 40:11

I, your Lord, will guide you continually, giving you water when you are dry and restoring your strength. You will be like a well-watered garden, like an ever-flowing spring. I will feed you, as My flock, like a Shepherd. I will carry you, My lamb, in My arms, holding you close to My Heart. I will gently lead My mother sheep along with her young.

FATHER, I choose to be thankful in good times and bad, as I realize your ever-present work in my life. I truly do need you, in all things and in every relationship, and in every circumstance in my life. I'm grateful that you have brought me through every day, into this path of intimacy with you. All I can say is let's keep going as it can only keep getting better. "Living a dedicated life" is the way to gain the "Light of Your Presence, Peace, and the gift of all gifts"! Yes! In Jesus' Name, Amen!

Psalm 32:8; Luke 10:41–42; Philippians 3:20–21

∽

I will guide you along the best pathway for your life. I'll communicate with you intimately, My advice, and I'll watch over you. As I said to My dear Martha, you are worried and upset over all the details! There is only one thing worth being concerned about, Mary has discovered it, and it will not be taken away. You are a citizen of heaven, where My Son Jesus lives. You are eagerly waiting for Him to return as your Savior. He will take your weak, mortal body and change it into a glorious body like His own. Then using the same power, He'll bring everything under His control.

FATHER, the only way out of natural responses is to live a life of relationship with a Supernatural God. I choose to live that life Lord, but without your constant intervention into my heart thoughts, I know I will not succeed, so in my own desire to believe and trust You I know I win! I make my conversations with You my first priority daily so that asking You, becomes my natural response. I love You Lord! In Jesus' Name, Amen!

Jeremiah 31:3;
Lamentations 3:25–26

~

Long ago, I, the Lord, said to Israel: "I have Loved you, My people, with an everlasting Love. With unfailing Love I have drawn you to Myself. I, the Lord, am good to those who depend upon Me, to those who search for Me. So it is good to wait quietly for the salvation, I give you. And it's also good to submit at an early age to the yoke of My discipline."

FATHER, I am so very grateful for my own relationship with You. Though the distractions are ever present, I choose to be engaged in You. I ask of You one thing today, and that is, whatever it takes to slow the distractions for the modern man, so that he can see past them to You. Though I am certain of You, he is not "yet." Let me, and those who will, carry Your Presence, Your Light, and Your Love to others, so that they may know You too. I ask you, my Lord, for Devine Appointments, today! In Jesus' Name, Amen!

Isaiah 9:6; John 20:21

❧

For unto you My Child is born, to you My Son is given.
The government will rest on His shoulders. He will be
called 'Wonderful Counselor, Mighty God, Everlasting
Father, Prince of Peace. 'My Peace be with you.' As I've sent
My Son, so I am sending You. I have breathed on You, now
receive the Holy Spirit.

FATHER, in every circumstance in life I choose Your Peace. I'm sure of this very thing, if You are not with me, I am lost. Help me to keep my mind on You so that Your Presence and Your Peace overshadow me all the days of my life. Breathe on me Lord, and fill me with Your Holy Spirit today. In Jesus' Name, Amen!

Ephesians 6:10–12

*Be strong in Me, and in My mighty Power. Put on My full
Armor so that you will be able to 'stand firm' against all
the strategies of the devil. For you do not fight against flesh
and blood, but against evil rulers of the unseen world, and
against evil powers in heavenly places.*

FATHER, You are where my help comes from. Your Name is high above all
else in my heart, and I place You in the highest place. I'm so grateful that I
can call upon Your Name at all times. You are my Great Defender from all
evil and I am blessed that when that day comes You will call me to "Stand."
I will Stand, because I have put my trust in You! You are my Hope and my
Salvation! In Jesus' Name, Amen!

Isaiah 55:8–9; Colossians 4:2; Psalm 116:17

❦

My thoughts are nothing like your thoughts, and My ways are far beyond anything you could imagine. For just as the heavens are higher than the earth, so My ways are higher than your ways and My thoughts higher than your thoughts. Devote yourself to intimate conversation with Me continually, with an alert mind and a thankful heart. Offer Me the sacrifice of thanksgiving, and call on My Name.

FATHER, I am so thankful for You. May our relationship continue to grow in intimate understanding and strength. You're always surprising me with Your Presence and participation in my day. Never stop! I truly need You, more and more. I feel that through the process, I'm also learning to love like You do! My heart for You, is causing My heart to gradually become Your heart toward others. That's amazing! And it's life changing too! "I love You Lord!" In Jesus' Name, Amen!

Psalm 31:20; Genesis 28:13

～

I hide you in the shelter of My Presence, safe from those who conspire against you, I shelter you in My Presence, far from accusing tongues. I Am your Lord, the God of your ancestors, Abraham and Isaac. The ground you are lying on belongs to you. I am giving it to you, and to your descendants.

FATHER, I pray that as you continue to train me to be aware of Your Presence, I'll learn to stay there. When life becomes too busy, I want to be so aware of You that when I'm doing whatever I must do, I'll stay aware of Your Presence around about me. For in that place, for me, is great delight and peace. In Jesus' Name, Amen!

Deuteronomy 6:5; Psalms 16:11

～

My child, love Me with all your heart, all your soul, and all your strength. You must commit yourself wholeheartedly to these commands that I am giving you today. I'll show you the way of Life, grant you the Joy of My Presence and the pleasure of living with Me forever.

FATHER, I will bless You with my life as I walk through this day. May all that I do, always bring You great Joy and Praise. As I walk my Life-path in Your Presence today, my focus will continually be on You, my Savior! In Jesus' Name, Amen!

Philippians 4:19; Colossians 2:2–3

❧

I, the same God who takes care of you will supply all your needs from My glorious riches, which have been given to you in Christ Jesus, My Son. Be encouraged and knit together by strong ties of Love. Have complete confidence that you'll understand God's mysterious plan, which is Christ Himself. In Him lie all the treasures of wisdom and knowledge.

FATHER, I thank You that You never fail to provide opportunity for me to grow in relationship with You. Your plan for My life is for good, and not ever for evil. I only need make the right choices to follow You and stay in Your Presence always. I do rejoice in all things that come my way, because I am convinced that You Lord, are in complete control! In Jesus' Name, Amen!

Psalm 23:4; Psalm 9:10; John 12:26

My Love, even when you walk through the darkest valley, you will not be afraid, because I Am close beside you. My rod and My staff protect you. I am a Shelter for the oppressed, a Refuge in times of trouble. Those who know My Name trust Me. I do not abandon those who search for Me. If you want to be My disciple, you must follow after Me, as My servant, be where I am. I will honor you if you serve Me.

FATHER, I choose to be fearless because of You. I know that my day is in Your hands and You have an excellent plan for me. My journey with You is always an adventure when I keep my focus on You. As we journey together through this day, I ask You for opportunities to share your Love with someone along the way. I'll be fearless, and do what You and I tenderly call "the stuff!" In Jesus' Name, Amen!

Isaiah 41:10; Psalm 139:9–10; James 1:2

*Yes, I, your Sovereign Lord am coming in Power! I rule
with a Powerful Arm. You see, I bring rewards with Me as
I come. If you ride the wings of the morning, if you dwell
by the farthest oceans, even there My Hand will guide you,
and My Strength will support you. When troubles come
your way, consider it an opportunity for My Great Joy!*

FATHER, I choose to keep my focus on You, so that my growth spiritually
will continue and my heart and life will become closer to You and more like
You daily. Even in the light of this, I realize that problems will come but I
will look for You and Your guidance in the midst of problems. As I know
that You are in them with me. I'll not be afraid, I know I will find Your Joy.
In Jesus' Name, Amen!

Psalms 36:9; Genesis 21:1, 7; Hebrews 11:1

~

For I Am the, "Fountain of Life," the 'Light' by which you see! I keep My Word; I did for Sarah, exactly what I promised, and gave Abraham a son in his old age. Faith is the confidence that what we hope for will actually happen; it gives us assurance about things we cannot see.

FATHER, I wait for the fulfillment of Your Words. Words I've received from Your Prophets. I'll be patient as I know that "Your timing is perfect" and that You're the Truth, my Lord, and the "Redeemer of Time." I believe You when You say: In You, "All things are Possible to those who believe." The journey is exciting when my heart is in a place of total surrender to You! That's where I want to stay, with my hope in You, always. In Jesus' Name, Amen!

II Thessalonians 1:10;
I Corinthians 6:19; Ephesians 3:20

～

When I return, on that day, I'll receive Glory from My holy people and praise from all who believe Me. This includes you, for you believed what you were told about Me. Don't you realize that your body is the Temple of the Holy Spirit, who Lives in you, and who was given to you by Me? You don't belong to yourself, but to Me, I bought you for a high price. So honor Me with your body. Remember that all Glory is to Me, for I Am able, by My Mighty Power at work within you, to accomplish infinitely more than you can ask or think.

FATHER, as I remain still, here in Your Presence now, cause my focus to be Your focus. May we be Face to face, and Heart to heart. I long to know You even more, and to know Your Ways more clearly. Help me Lord, to have clean hands and a pure heart before You. And fill me, Lord, with Your Holy Spirit so that I might honor You with everything I am and with every fiber of my being. My desire is to serve You completely. Let Your dreams be my very own dreams. And, then, may You receive all Glory, Honor, and Praise through my life today. In Jesus' Name, Amen!

Romans 8:23–25; Hebrews 6:19–20

❧

My child you groan, even though you have My Holy Spirit within as a foretaste of future Glory. You long for your body to be released from all sin and suffering. You wait with eager hope for the day that I will give you your full right as My adopted child, including your new body that I promised. You were given this hope when you were saved, remember this and don't be anxious. This hope is a strong and trustworthy anchor for your soul. It leads you through the curtain into the inner sanctuary. Jesus already went in there for you, Your eternal High Priest.

FATHER, as I sit here, in the early morning hours, peering out the window to the still-dark morning, there is a light blanket of snow on the ground which makes it look, oh so cold and yet clean. There is *hope in my heart* that Your plans and purposes are on the way. They'll arrive just at the right moment, bringing with them the answers that will brighten my spiritual understanding of Your will for my needs and concerns. My *hope* is in You alone My Lord, and I know Your Love for me is never-ending. *Heaven is my destination!* In Jesus' Name, Amen!

Isaiah 50:4; Revelation 2:3; Isaiah 60:2

❧

I, your Sovereign Lord, have given you My Words of wisdom, so that you know how to comfort the weary. Morning by morning I awaken you and open your understanding to My will. You've patiently suffered for Me without quitting. Darkness covers all the nations of the earth, but My Glory rises and appears over you.

My Savior, I long to spend more time with You. My desire is to be a true blessing every day of my life. In doing this, my life changes day by day, and moment by moment; *this I love.* If I submit to You, and Your Words of wisdom are in me, then I'll know how to comfort others for You. Then I too will have even more freedom from the darkness of this world. This is Your way for my life, and for that I am truly blessed by You. Lord, You're my highest priority; help me by Your Spirit, to stay focused on Your Presence and Your leading today. In Jesus' Name, Amen!

II Corinthians 4:6; Colossians 2:9–10; Psalm 150:6

~

I, your God, say; "Let there be Light in the darkness." I've made this Light to shine in your heart, so that you could know My Glory that is seen in the Face of Jesus. Know this, that this Light shines in your heart, but you yourself are like a fragile jar of clay containing this great treasure. This makes it clear that your great power is from Me, not from you yourself. For in Jesus is all My fullness in a human body. So you yourself are complete through your union with Jesus, who is the head over every ruler and authority. Let everything that has breath, Praise Me, The Lord of all!

FATHER, "Praise You, from whom all blessings flow. Praise You, all creatures here below. Praise You, above the heavenly host. Praise Father, Son, and Holy Ghost! Amen." Thank You, my God, for Your Son, my Jesus. As Your Light shines in Him, let it also shine through Him in me, Your servant. I am amazed at Your goodness and kindness. I'm completed in the knowledge of Your Love, Mercy, and Grace that causes Your Light to fill me up with overwhelming Joy and great Peace, so that I can represent, in union with Jesus, Your great Love to others, today. In Jesus' Name, Amen!

Isaiah 30:20–21; II Corinthians 4:17

～

*My Love, though I gave you adversity for food, and suffering
for drink, I'll be with you to teach you. You'll see Me, your
teacher, with your own eyes. Your own ears will hear Me.
Right behind you, My voice will say; "This is the way you
should go," whether to the right or to the left. For your
present troubles are small and won't last very long., yet they
produce in you My Glory, that vastly outweighs them, and
will last forever.*

FATHER, as I change from complaining to You about problems that come
my way, to looking for where You are in the midst of them, they become an
adventure, an assignment with You, instead of a separation from You in my
own heart. Oh, it is awesome to see things in life from Your perspective.
They are then never overwhelming or impossible to overcome. I realize *I
really am "More than a Conqueror" in You!* In Jesus' Name, Amen!

Proverbs 16:2–3; Matthew 6:31–34

⟫

My child, what is your heart's motive? Commit your actions to Me, and your plans will succeed. Don't worry about what you'll eat, drink, or wear. These things dominate the thoughts of unbelievers, but I already know your needs. Seek My Kingdom, above all else, live righteously, and I'll give you everything you need. Don't worry or fret about tomorrow, for tomorrow will bring its own worries. Today's trouble is enough for today.

FATHER, in this season of my life, it seems the list of "to do's" is much longer than is normal. As long as I keep my focus on You, my King, in this place of closeness with You, I can accomplish everything. You remind me intimately of what's important for me to get done today. I ask You Lord, to teach me to know how to be *"in this world but not of it"* in the way that You originally intended me to be! Then my days will be fulfilling and my walk with You complete but without this world's concerns. I'll continually trust You in every circumstance of my life, today and always. In Jesus' Name, Amen!

Psalm 92:1–5; Psalm 95:6–8

❧

It is good to give thanks and to sing praises to Me, your Lord Most High. It is good to proclaim My unfailing Love in the morning, and My Faithfulness in the evening, accompanied by the ten-stringed harp and the melody of the lyre. I thrill you with all I have done for you, and cause you to sing for Joy because of all I've done. Great works I've done, and how deep are my thoughts. Come, worship, bow down, kneel before Me; I Am the Lord your Maker. I Am your God, and you're the people I watch over, the flock under My care. If only you'd 'listen to My Voice!'

FATHER, I've known the Love that's within You for the people in the world. I've had opportunities to experience that Love when in the midst of "divine appointments" that You've provided me with when I've asked to be Your heart, and a reflection of You to others. I listen to You, and desire to know You and Your Love more! So, I say, Lord, I surrender my whole life to you again, to be used as You will. Let Your Presence so dwell in and through me, that I may reach as many as possible with Your Salvation. All praise be unto You, always and forever! In Jesus' Name, Amen!

Luke 4:18–19; Psalm 63:2; II Corinthians 5:7–8

~

"My Spirit is upon you, for I've anointed you to bring Good News to the poor. I've sent you to proclaim that captives be released, that the blind will see, that the oppressed will be set free, and the Favor of the Lord, Come!" You've seen Me within My Sanctuary, and you've gazed upon My Power and Glory. For you Live by believing and not by seeing. Yes, you are fully confident, and would rather be away from your earthly body, for then you would be at home with Me.

FATHER, I expect to see Your Glory, Miracles, Power, and Fire, in the Name of Jesus! I believe that the days ahead hold things that no man can know or even think. I choose to depend on You Lord, and trust You to use me in Your plans, all the days of my life. Our intimacy is growing continually as You are transforming me from darkness to Your glorious Light. I believe Your Love for me is perfect, and that, when I am weak, You Lord are always Strong. I know that I'm highly favored of You, and I'm fully confident in You. I say, "Yes," as I know that You are sending me to preach the Good News to the poor and needy. You Lord are with me, and You anoint me, protect and comfort me, everyday. One day I will reign with You eternally. Hallelujah! In Jesus' Name, Amen!

John 1:14; Luke 1:76–79

≈

Jesus My Son, The Word, became human and made His home among you. Jesus, is so full of unfailing Love and Faithfulness! You've seen His Glory, the Glory of My Only Son. Jesus, My Son, shall be called the Prophet of the Most High, He'll prepare the way! He'll tell His people how to find salvation through forgiveness of their sins. Because of My tender Mercy, the morning Light from heaven is about to break upon you, to give out Light to those who sit in darkness and in the shadow of death. To guide you on My Path of Peace.

FATHER, Son, and Holy Spirit. I'm so grateful for my understanding of who You truly are, *Three in One*. Though my understanding is minimal, of the vastness of Your truth. I'm in awe of Your concern for me. I know Your Love for me is greater than my love for You. And when I think of all You've done for me, I'm broken, and elated in the depths of my heart. My entire life is surrendered to You completely, in order to express my gratitude if its possible for any human to express. I'll serve and Love You all the days of my life, and into eternity! In Jesus' Name, Amen!

I Timothy 6:15–16; Romans 8:32; II Peter 1:18–19

~

My child, at the right time, Christ Jesus My Son will be revealed to you from heaven by Me, your Almighty God, the King of all kings, and Lord of all lords. He can never die; He Lives in Light so brilliant that no human can approach Him. No human eyes have ever seen Him, and never will. All Honor and Power to Him forever! Since I didn't spare My Own Son, but gave Him up for all, won't I also give You everything else? He paid the ransom to save you from the empty life you inherited from your ancestors. The ransom paid was not mere gold or silver. It was the precious blood of Christ Jesus, My Son, the sinless, and spotless Lamb.

FATHER, I'm so grateful that You, my Lord, are my very closest Friend. I find myself closer to you, than any other. This is the best place I've found for me. In Your Presence is where I receive all that I need to do just what You desire of me. Let Your Light Shine in me, to the people I meet along my life-path, so that they will desire more of You! As the Light of the world, we the church, in obedience to You can fulfill Your heart's desire. Thank you Father, for sending Your Son, Jesus, my Savior. Come, by Your blood, and by the word of my testimony. Live in and through my life today. In Jesus' Name, Amen!

Psalm 90:2; Colossians 1:27; Colossians 3:15, 17

≈

Before the mountains were born, before I gave birth to the earth and the world, from beginning to end, I Am your God. I want all to know that the riches and Glory of Christ are for the Gentiles too. This is the secret: Christ Lives in you. This gives you the assurance of sharing His Glory. Let the Peace that comes from Christ rule in your hearts. For as members of One body, you are called to live in Peace. And always be thankful. Whatever you do or say, do it as a representative of the Lord Jesus, giving thanks through Him to Me, the Father.

FATHER, I'm so very thankful for Your plan for my life. You're all that I need to live, and those times "in silence," when You speak to me in the depths of my being, are what I live for. You Lord, are my hope! Your Presence is glorious and I'm at perfect Peace, filled with thankfulness as I ponder the salvation You came to give me. May I live in this reality daily, in remembrance of You. Then Your Love will flow from me to others, and Your plan will be fulfilled in my life, abundantly. In Jesus' Name, Amen!

I John 4:15–19; Psalm 13:5–6

Confess that Jesus is My Son, then I Live in you, and you Live in Me. You know how much I Love you, and you put your trust in My Love. I Am Love; you who live in love, Live in Me, and I Live in you. As you Live in Me, our Love grows more perfect. You will not be afraid on the day of judgment, but you can face Me with complete confidence, because you Live like Jesus here in this world. Such Love has no fear, because perfect Love expels all fear. If you're afraid it is for fear of punishment, and this shows that you have not fully experienced My perfect Love. Love each other because I Loved you first. Trust in My unfailing Love, rejoice because I've rescued you. Sing to Me, because I Am Good to you.

FATHER, be with me as I walk with You through this day. Cause me to see You and Your Love for me in the midst of it all. Thank You, Lord, for family; may Your Peace fill my home as I gather together with others. For those who may be alone, I pray that Your Presence would fill the air around them and they would know You and Your Love completely. Bring revelation to my heart today, for Your Name's sake above all else. The greatest gift of all is in Jesus, the Salvation that You Give so Freely today. I put my trust in You Lord now. Your unconditional Love is mine, and You Sing over me with that Love. You're so Good to me. In Jesus' Name, Amen!

II Corinthians 4:6–7; Luke 2:14; II Corinthians 8:9

For I, your God say; "Let there be Light in the darkness." I've made My Light to Shine in your heart, so you could know My Glory, which is seen on the Face of Jesus. You now have this Light Shining in your heart, you're like a fragile clay jar containing My Great Treasure. It's clear that your great power is from Me, not of yourself. Give to Me your Glory, your God in the highest heaven. Then there'll be Peace on earth for you, if you give Me all your honor. You know the generous grace of Jesus, though He's rich, for your sake He became poor, that by His poverty He could make you Rich in Him.

FATHER, I chose to sing my Praises to Your Name. I ponder all the wondrous Glory of You, and all You've done for Me! I think of these days in which I live, and how I see You in my daily life. All that You've accomplished in me, is amazing and I'm awed by it all. I think of the things that You've revealed to me, of a future and a hope. I'm in a place of anticipation, as I rest in You intentionally, knowing You're at the forefront of my life-path, and yet You're surrounding me. I follow You now, trusting You every step of the way! I lean into You, and simply breath You in. I snuggle into Your Peace, and the comfort of Your amazing Love! In Jesus' Name, Amen!

Isaiah 64:4; John 15:16–19; Proverbs 21:21

❧

Since the world began, no ear has heard, and no eye has seen a God like Me. I work for you who 'wait' on Me. You didn't chose Me, I choose You. I've appointed You to 'Go' and produce lasting fruit, so that I, your Father, will give to you whatever you ask for, using My Name. This is My commandment; Love each other. If the world hates you, remember that it hated Me first. The world doesn't love you because you're not part of it. Pursue righteousness and unfailing Love and you'll find Life, Righteousness, and Honor.

FATHER, as I sit here in my quiet home this day, I turn off all earthly sound and tune my heart's ear toward heaven. As I snuggle into this place, I know what is awaiting me here is time with You. I also know that this time is more than necessary to prepare me for the day ahead, and for the future. I spend time in your Word, because I know that Your Word is Life for me. Your Word and the teaching of the Holy Spirit fill me with all the knowledge I need to ward off the enemies that may try to enter my day, or the day of others I'll meet along the way. I choose to be prepared, to be ready to do "the stuff" in your plan for my day. I give thanks to You Lord, for my Life today. In Jesus' Name, Amen!

Psalm 40:4–5; Psalm 56:10–11; Isaiah 26:2–4

∼

Oh the Joy that is yours when you put your trust in Me. Have no confidence in the proud or in those who worship idols. I've performed many wonders for you. My plans for you are too numerous to list. I have no equal. If you tried to recite all of My Wondrous deeds, you would never come to an end of them. I'll open the gates to you who are righteous, and I'll allow the faithful to enter in. Praise Me, for what I have promised you. You trust Me, so why be afraid? What can people really do to you? I'll keep you in perfect Peace as you put your trust in Me. Fix your thoughts on Me, Trust Me always. I Am your Lord, and your eternal Rock.

FATHER, my trust in You has grown, along side of my constant desire to know You more. In Your Word I find all the truth I need to hold fast to my faith in You. My consistency with You is my greatest witness to others. You've told me so. In my walk with You, I find our intimate conversational relationship continues to grow deeper moment by moment, each day. Your Light and Love permeate my entire being, then funnel through me to others. Open the ancient gates, and cause my spiritual senses to be awakened to You more today. I've centered my heart on You, my Rock and my Salvation. It is in You, I've put all of my trust. I Love You intentionally. You're my eternal Savior. In Jesus' Name, Amen!

II Corinthians 5:17; Ephesians 2:8–10; I John 4:7–8

～

My beloved, if you belong to My Son Jesus, you've become a new person. The old life is gone, Your New Life has begun. I saved you by My Grace when you believed. You cannot take credit for this, it's a gift from Me. Salvation is not a reward for the good things you've done, so no one can boast about it. You are My masterpiece. I created you 'New in Christ Jesus, My Son.' You can now do the good things I planned for you long ago.

Beloved, continually love others, for this Love comes from Me. Love as a child of Mine who knows Me. If you don't love others, you don't know Me, because I Am Love!

FATHER, I do Love You! And I'm so thankful for the journey You have me on. I'm thankful that You Lord, are with Me all the way. I rest in the fact that whatever comes my way, *You and I together* can handle! I pray that Your gifts of wisdom and discernment grow deeper in me every day. I want to recognize clearly the hurts and needs of others. I want to be Your Voice, Your Heart of Love, to bring many closer to You, *and to please You always*! I'm thankful for the Holy Spirit who draws my heart to You. I love the assurance that the work is being done in and through me, as I lose myself in You. I enjoy all of the adventures You bring into my life continually. I Love You! Here I am, Lord, send me. In Jesus' Name, Amen!

II Corinthians 2:14–17

❧

Thank Me, My beloved. I made you My captive and I continue to lead you along Christ's triumphal procession. Now I use you to spread the knowledge of Christ Jesus My Son everywhere, like a sweet perfume. Your life is a Christ-Like fragrance rising up to Me Your God. This fragrance is perceived differently by those who are being Saved and those who are perishing. To those who are perishing, you're a dreadful smell of death and doom, but, to those who are being Saved, you're a Life-giving perfume.

Who is adequate for such a task as this? You see, you're not like the many hucksters who preach for personal profit. You preach My Word with sincerity and with Christ's authority, knowing that I Am watching you.

FATHER, I Thank You for all You've accomplished in Me. For all You've taught me, and all You've brought me through. I look forward, with great anticipation, to what You have in mind for the days ahead. I pray I will lean on You and stick closer to You than ever before. I know the safety and peace that are there in that place of comfort and learning to be transformed. I pray that our intimate conversational relationship will continue to grow day by day. And that I'll receive from You a deeper understanding of Your Word, and a deep hunger for it. I realize that the desire to do Your will, must be coupled with Your Word, and I need to understand and discern it. I must apply Your Word to every part of Your call on my life. In Jesus' Name, Amen!

Romans 12:2, 9–10; Jeremiah 29:11–13

My child, don't copy the behaviors and customs of this world, but let Me transform you into a new person by changing the way you think. Then you'll learn to know My will for you, which is good and pleasing and perfect. Don't just pretend to love others. Really Love them! Hate what is wrong. Hold tightly to what is good. Love each other with genuine affection, and take delight in honoring each other. For I know the plans I have for you; they are plans for good and not for disaster, to give you a future and a hope. When you pray, I'll listen. If you look for Me with your whole heart, you will find Me.

FATHER GOD, I look forward to the days ahead, knowing full well they'll be life-changing, and filled with unknowing challenges and adventures with You. I'll continually keep my mind focused on You. One thing I'm sure of is that You have my days in Your hands and they are already planned. You Lord, are in control of all things. Nothing that comes my way is a surprise to You. My hope is that my heart's responses will be a blessing to You; that my choices will bring Joy to Your heart and give You praise. You, my King, have full reign to bring about transformation in me. I want to be a reflection of You! Change me Lord, and take delight in me always. I thank You Father, from the depths of my heart for all things, today. In My Jesus' Name, Amen!

Psalm 105:1–5; Psalm 108:1–5

❧

*Give Me thanks, and proclaim My Greatness! Let the
whole world know what I've done. Sing to Me; Yes, sing My
Praises. Tell everyone about My wonderful deeds. Exult in
My Holy Name; Rejoice, you who worship Me. Search for
Me, and for My Strength: continually seek Me. Remember
the wonders I have performed, My Miracles and the rulings
I've given. Give thanks to Me among all the people. You'll
sing praises to Me among the nations. My unfailing Love
is higher than the heavens. My faithfulness reaches to the
clouds. Exalt Me, your God, above the highest heavens, and
My Glory shines over all the earth.*

FATHER, I desire more time with You. I know that the more time I spend
with You, the stronger I become to face this world and its evil ways. In any
way You call upon me, I say, "Yes Lord!" I want more of Your equipping
in my life, and I know that with You all things are possible! I choose to be
positive and filled with faith in my heart, no matter what the circumstances
might be. Nothing is more important than You! In Jesus' Mighty Name,
Amen!

Psalm 31:19–20; John 16:33

෭

*How great is the Goodness I've stored up for those who
fear Me. I lavish it on you, who come to Me for protection,
blessing you before a watching world. I hide you in the
shelter of My Presence, safe from those who conspire
against you. I shelter you in My Presence, far from accusing
tongues. Praise Me, for I've shown you the wonders of My
unfailing Love. I keep you safe when your cities are under
attack. I've told you all this so you'll have peace in Me. Here
on earth you'll have many trials and sorrows, but take heart,
because I've Overcome the world.*

FATHER, I thank You for the amazing Peace and Love that comes when
I put my trust in You, surrendering to Your willingness to carry all my difficulties. You alone have the answers and are completely capable of figuring
them out. I will not doubt Your abilities, and though I may stress at times,
I'll consult Your wisdom and guidance in every situation that comes my
way, good or bad. I choose to give You all of my burdens and my heart of
faith and Love forever. For You keep me in perfect Peace as I keep my mind
focused on You and I stay in intimate communion with You, abiding in Your
awesome Presence. In Jesus' Name, Amen!

Isaiah 40:10–11; Isaiah 41:10, 13

❧

*I, your Sovereign Lord am Coming! I'll Rule with a Powerful
Arm. See, I bring My reward with Me as I Come. I feed
My flock like a Shepherd. I carry the Lambs in My Arms,
holding them close to My Heart. I gently lead the mother
sheep with her young. Don't be afraid, for I Am with you.
Don't allow yourself to be discouraged, I Am your God.
I strengthen you and help you. I hold you up with My
Victorious Right Hand. I hold you by your right hand,
I Am the Lord your God. And I say to you, do not be afraid,
I Am here to help you.*

MY FATHER, in heaven, may Your Name be kept Holy. May Your Kingdom soon come. May Your will be done, on earth, as it is in heaven. Give me
today the food I need, and forgive me, my sins, as I've forgiven those who've
sinned against me. Don't let me yield to temptation, but rescue me from the
evil one. For Yours is the Kingdom, the Power, and the Glory forever. I'll not
be discouraged because You're my God. Your Strength is my Joy! You never
leave my side. You encompass me with Your Presence continually. I am
Yours. You prove it to me in outrageous ways every day. In the intimacy of
the moment, I find that You're there, listening, for me. In Jesus' Name, Amen!

II Corinthians 4:16–18;
Job 38:34–37; Job 32:8, 9

❧

My beloved, this is why you 'never give up!' Your body is dying, but your spirit is being renewed daily. Your present troubles are small and won't last long. Yet they produce for you a glory that vastly outweighs them and will last forever! So don't look at the troubles you can see now; rather, fix your gaze on things that cannot be seen. For the things you see now will soon be gone. The things you cannot see will last forever. I can shout to the clouds and make it rain. I can make lightning appear and cause it to strike as I direct. I give intuition to the heart and instinct to the mind. I Am Wise enough to count all the clouds. I tilt the water jars of heaven. My Spirit is within you, My Almighty breath within you makes you intelligent. Sometimes the elders are not wise. The aged do not understand justice sometimes.

FATHER GOD, I thank you for teaching me, day by day, to recognize my need to depend on You in every situation in my life. My own marriage, has been a place of learning this very thing, for both of us. Today, being in years of marriage, I look back over the years of many trials, tribulations, twists, and turns I know that every one of them were times of strengthening both of our relationships, with You first, and then with each other. Your Word tells us that You'll never leave us, or forsake us, and I'm grateful. I know that without You, no marriage, or any relationship, can ever be a success. I'm thankful Lord, You walked with me in the good times, and the bad times, too. You, Father, have been my God, Jesus my Savior, and Holy Spirit my teacher throughout all time. I've known Your Love, and your Love for others, also. Thank You for calling me unto yourself. We've needed You every day. In Jesus' Name, Amen!

Ephesians 3:20–21; Romans 8:1–2; Isaiah 40:31

~

My child, All Glory be unto Me. I Am able, through My Mighty Power at work within you, to accomplish infinitely more than you might ask or think. Glory be to Me, in the church and in Jesus, My Son, through all generations forever and ever! Remember, there is no condemnation for you, if you belong to My Son, Jesus. Because you belong to Him, the Power of My Life-giving Spirit has freed you from the power of sin and death. You, who trust in Me, will find new strength. You'll soar high on wings like eagles. You'll run and not grow weary, you'll walk and not faint.

FATHER, it is fantastic to me that the longer and closer I walk with You the more aware I am of Your Presence and Your desire for more of a participation in my personal and interactive life. You're truly alive and full of Love for me, and for those I love. I'll trust You and watch as You make me more aware of You and of Your direction in my life, and our intimate conversations concerning every situation of my life. I ask You for greater discernment and wisdom to know, Your deepest heart desires! I long to continually please You in all I do. In Jesus' Name, Amen!

Psalm 22:3–5; Psalm 146:1–2; I Thessalonians 5:16–18

❧

I Am Holy, enthroned on the Praises of Israel. Your ancestors trusted in Me, and I rescued them. They cried out to Me, and were saved; trusted in Me and were never disgraced. Let all that you are Praise Me! Praise Me, your Lord, as long as you live. Sing your Praises to Me until your dying breath. Always be Joyful! Never stop praying. Be thankful in every circumstance, for this is My will for you, in Jesus, My Son. Do not stifle the Holy Spirit. Do not scoff at prophecies, but test all that is said. Hold on to what is good!

FATHER, today I choose to fill my heart and mind with all the reasons I need to be and am thankful for Your Love for me. I realize that some things are harder than others to be thankful for, but You Lord, are completely aware of way more than I know and "You're in control of it all." I'll take my own thoughts captive, and redirect them to You and Your many blessings in my life. I'll spend more time in your Word and intimately talking with You about all that concerns me. I'll continually thank You and praise You for what You have done, continually do, and for who You are, my King! In Jesus' Name, Amen!

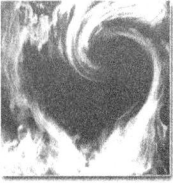

Psalm 46:1–2; Romans 12:12–15; Romans 15:13

~

My child, I Am your Refuge and Strength, always ready to help in your time of trouble. Do not fear when earthquakes come and the mountains crumble into the sea. Rejoice in your confident Hope! Be patient in trouble, and keep on praying. When My people are in need, be ready to help them. Always be eager to practice hospitality. Bless those who persecute you. Don't curse them. Pray that I'll bless them. Be happy with those who are happy, and weep with those who weep. Pray that I, your source of hope, will fill you completely with Joy and Peace because you trust in Me. Then you'll overflow with confident hope through the Power of the Holy Spirit!

FATHER GOD, all of my hope is in You, and in You alone. I learn more about Your Love for me every day. I've realized that Your ways are the opposite of the world's ways. I see that knowing this and learning of You through Your Word, brings greater insight to the ways of the enemy. I'm completely aware of my own inadequacies, and my need for a deeper dependence on my intimate conversational relationship with You. You're my gentle and loving Savior, my hope, and faith are in You alone. I'm learning to walk in patience, goodness, kindness, gentleness, and self-control. I'm learning to trust You, and Love You with every fiber of my being. My confidence in You and in myself has grown stronger and I know that the Holy Spirit is my Comfort. He'll be my teacher, and I'll remain teachable until I breathe my last breath. In Jesus' Name, Amen!

Proverbs 3:1–8; Psalm 40:3

My child, never forget the things I've taught you. Store My commands in your heart. If you do this, you'll live many years and your life will be satisfying. Never let loyalty and kindness leave you! Tie them around your neck as a reminder. Write them deep within your heart. Then you'll find favor with Me, and others, and you'll earn a good reputation. Trust in Me with all your heart; do not depend on your own understanding. Seek My will in all you do, and I'll show you which path to take. Don't be impressed with your own wisdom. Instead, fear Me and turn away from evil. Then you'll have healing for your body and strength for your bones.

FATHER, I choose to trust You, to trust Your decisions and Your timing in every circumstance I encounter. I know that nothing can stop me, as long as I stay in Your will. *I'll never give up!* I'll conquer any discouragement that comes my way. I'll stay in close, and intimate communion with You my Savior. I trust that Your timing is perfect and You're the Redeemer of time. I believe in You with all my heart, for I've experienced wrong timing because of my anxious ways. I'm changing and learning to trust that your ways are definitely way higher than mine. I'll trust You, my Lord, with all of my heart, for Your wisdom, healing, and strength. In Jesus' Name, Amen!

Romans 12:2, 9–10;
Jeremiah 29:11–13

~

My beloved, don't copy the behavior and customs of this world, but let Me transform you into a new person by changing the way you think. Then you'll learn to know My Will for you, which is good and pleasing and perfect. Don't just pretend to love others. Really love them! Hate what is wrong. Hold tightly to what is good, and Love others with genuine affection, take delight in honoring each other. For I know the plans I have for you, plans for good and not disaster, to give you a future and a hope. When you pray, I'll listen. If you look for Me with your spiritual eyes, I'll be found by you.

FATHER, I have the greatest goal in this life, and that is to remain teachable until I breathe my very last breath! I'm aware of my need to learn more. My desire is to become that Bride without spot or wrinkle. Ready and waiting for her Groom! I realize I have a long way to go, but, in Your Presence I Believe *'all things are possible!'* I'll keep my focus on You this year, even more than the last; with a deeper desire to bring pleasure to You than to myself or to others. I'll be a *'Risk Taker'* when I know that You're prompting me. *'Fearless and Ready to Stand!'* I'll be listening to Your still small, yet tremendous, voice. You'll find me watching for *'Your Heart'* in the center of every situation. How exciting it is to be Yours, and to serve You today! In Jesus' Name, Amen!

Psalm 31:19–20; John 16:33; Proverbs 16:1–3

~

How great is the goodness I have stored up for you who fear Me. I lavish it on you, because you come to Me for protection. I bless you before a watching world. I hide you in the shelter of My Presence, safe from those who may conspire against you; sheltering you within My Presence, far from accusing tongues. I tell you this, so that you may have Peace in Me. Here on earth, you'll have many trials and sorrows' but take heart, I've overcome the world. You can choose and make your own plans, but I'll give you the right answers. You may be pure in your own eyes, but I examine your heart's motive. Commit your choices and actions to Me, and your plans will succeed.

FATHER, in Your strong yet gentle Presence, I'm refreshed and renewed. Your Peace fills my heart, and stays there through the day. When I'm hidden in You, I know the meaning and value of Your Peace in my very existence. My heart is filled with sounds and vibrations of worship. My spirit sings of Your matchlessness. This is where I become more aware of what Your unconditional Love is. I receive it! I know You're my constant companion, and that our intimate relationship grows as You dwell within me, speaking to me through the whole day. As I walk this journey of life, I pray that You'll be obvious to others, through me. Let Your peace in my heart, infect them, and bring other's lives to the Peace that only You can give. Your Peace is what many unknowingly need so desperately, today! In Jesus' Name, Amen!

Isaiah 40:10–11, 28–31

～

*Yes, my beloved, I, Your Sovereign Lord, Am Coming
in Power! I Rule with a Powerful arm. You see, I bring
My Reward with Me as I Come. I'll feed My flock like a
Shepherd. I'll carry you, My lamb in My arms. I'll hold you
close to My heart. I'll gently lead the mother sheep with her
young. Have you heard, and have you understood? I Am
the Everlasting God, the Creator of all the earth. I never
grow weak or weary. No one can measure the depths of My
understanding. I give power to the weak and strength to the
powerless. Even all the youth will become weak and tired,
and young men will fall in exhaustion. But, trust in Me and
you'll find new strength, you'll soar high on wings like eagles.
You'll run and not grow weary, walk and not grow faint.*

LORD, it's my desire to *trust You completely*. I'm learning to in the midst of everyday events. Sometimes knowing that without Your intervention and wisdom, I would lose it, and fail. I know that You're my great Hope! My faith is expanded when I watch You take part in my daily life, and in the lives of those around me. You're ultimately in control of everything that concerns me, or those I know and love. You're my awesome example of unconditional Love. You show me Your Mercy and Grace when I feel so undeserving. Your extended hand of help is always there for the taking. Teach me Lord, to be more aware of how easily I can reach out and take hold of Your hand, finding there Your secure and lasting Peace for today. In Jesus' Name, I put my trust, Amen!

II Corinthians 5:9–10; Psalm 53:1–2; Psalm 56:11–13

My beloved, whether you're here in this body, or away from this body, your goal is to be to please Me. For you'll all stand before Christ Jesus to be judged. You'll receive whatever you deserve; the good or evil you've done in this earthly body. Only a fool says in his heart there's no God, they are evil and do no good. I look down from heaven on the entire human race to see if anyone is truly wise, if anyone seeks after Me. You trust Me, so why should you be afraid? Fulfill your vow to Me, your God. Offer a sacrifice of Praise for My help. I've rescued you from death, and I've kept your feet from slipping. Now, you can walk in My Presence, in My Life-giving Light.

LORD, I deeply depend on You. I've tried on my own and learned that without You 'I can do nothing of real eternal value' for myself or for others. I've learned that when I fall or fail, You are there. Even when I make a mistake, You make a way to correct it, when I humbly take the lower place. You, Lord, are my Defender, as well as my Best Friend, and my Teacher. I come to You with my heart and my mind open, and eager to learn the many things You'll teach me, as we walk together along this blessed journey called life. I'll remain teachable and walk close by Your side. Victorious in all circumstances. As I trust Your ways and not my own, I'm filled and refreshed. I deeply depend on You, always. In Jesus' Way and Name, Amen!

Ephesians 3:20–21; Romans 8:6

❧

Now all Glory is Mine! I Am able through My Mighty Power, at work within you, to accomplish infinitely more than you may ask or think. Glory be to Me, in the church and in My Son Jesus, through all generations forever and ever! By letting your sinful nature control your mind, it leads to death. But letting My Spirit control your mind leads to Life, and Peace. Your sinful nature is always hostile to Me. It has never obeyed My laws, and it never will. That's why those who are still under the control of their sinful nature can never please Me. So simply <u>Surrender</u>!

LORD, I come to You quietly, to draw close and to hear from You. I am feeling down today. Some things are far beyond my ability to understand, and I need Your Spirit to comfort me. I've put my trust in You, and soak up the Peace that's within Your Presence. I ask You to take control of my thoughts so that I can focus on You and Your Word today. I know in time I'll learn to understand Your plans and purposes. Help me to wait and to rest in Your truth that's in me already. I'll not worry, but I'll put my trust in You for Your' Outrageous Outcome.' You've ordained Peace for my life-path. Your Grace and Glory are mine for the asking, and the Peace that passes all earthly understanding is here, now. My heart's mind and eyes are watching for You as I wait for time to pass. I'll join with others who are in need of Your touch today; encouraging others in Your abiding Love today. As I 'surrender to You.' In Jesus' Name, Amen!

Psalm 22:30–31; Psalm 146:1–2; I Thessalonians 5:16–18

My beloved, your children will also serve Me. Future generations will hear about My many wonders. My Righteous acts will be told to those not yet born. They'll hear about everything I've done. Praise Me! Let all that you are, and can be, Praise My Name! Praise Me as long as you live! You'll sing Praise to Me with your dying breath. Don't put your confidence in powerful people: for there's no help for you there. Always be Joyful! Never stop talking to Me! Thank Me in every circumstance of life, for this is My will for you. You belong to Me!

LORD GOD, my hope is in You, and in You alone I put my trust. I'm so thankful for You Lord, in every portion of my life. I'll remain thankful in all circumstances, and continually give You all of my heart-felt Praise. In times of difficulty, and in times of joy, I can not imagine not having Your Presence to lean into. Your Name is all that my heart can utter in surrender when my deepest need is there. I sing my Praises to You with sheer Joy. I have the eternal pleasure of knowing You as my Savior and King. Lord, discipline my heart to fill the empty moments of my life with intimate times of conversation and Praises unto You. Words filled with thanksgiving I speak out unto You in Your amazing Presence. In Jesus' Name, Amen!

Psalm 46:1, 10–11; Romans 12:12–13; Romans 15:13

I, your God Am your Refuge and Strength, always ready to help when you have trouble. Be still and know that I Am your God! I'll be honored by every nation throughout the world. I, the 'Lord of Heavens Armies,' Am here for you. I, the 'God of Israel,' Am your Fortress. Rejoice in confident hope. Be patient in trouble, and keep intimately conversing with Me. When My people are in need, be ready to help them. Always be eager to be hospitable. Pray that I, your Source of all Hope, will fill you completely with My Joy and Peace, because you trust in Me. Then you'll overflow with more confident hope through the Power of My Holy Spirit.

LORD, I'm encompassed by Your Presence when I sit quietly with You. Your tender loving mercy, and Your intimate Grace are mine in the weakness of my own personal needs. In my times of troubles, You Lord, lift me up. I can feel the Strength in the Joyfulness of Your heart. I put my confident hope in You alone. I know that in my intimate conversational communion with You, I'll find that all things are possible because I believe in You. In the deep darkness of this world, Your sweet Presence provides the Light I need. I'll cling tightly to You, for You Lord, are my greatest Hope; my Everything, completely! In Jesus' Name, Amen!

Colossians 4:2–6; II Peter 1:10–11

≈

My beloved, devote yourself to prayer with an alert mind and thankful heart. Pray for others, that I'll give you opportunities to speak to them about My mysterious plan concerning Christ. That is why you're a servant. Pray that you'll proclaim this message as clearly as is possible. Live wisely among those who are not yet believers, and make the most of every opportunity. Let your conversation be gracious and attractive, so you'll have the right response for everyone. Work hard to prove that you really are among those I've called and chosen. Do these things, and you'll never fall away. Then I'll give you a grand entrance into the eternal Kingdom of My Son, your Lord, Savior, and Bridegroom, Jesus Christ.

LORD, I believe You hear my heart of prayer as I share all that concerns me. I believe You're at work on my behalf, even before I've asked, because You know my every need. It's difficult to remember when tragedies or tensions arise that You're always there in the midst of it all. You're completely aware and strategizing on my behalf. *You're in control!* When I share with You my hearts dreams, You're waiting for my faith to arise. In the whole process, You're transforming me into your likeness. My trust in You is being made complete, and if I chose to believe. I'll be able to watch You in the process. I'll experience Your Wisdom and Light in the outcome. Through it all, Your Mercy, Grace, and Love are mine, today and everyday. In Jesus' Name, Amen!

Exodus 33:14, 17; John 15:4–7

~

My beloved, "I'll personally go with you, and give you rest. Everything will be fine for you." "I'll indeed do what you've asked, for I look favorably on you. I know you by name." Remain in Me, and I'll remain in you. For a branch cannot produce fruit if it is severed from the vine, and you cannot be fruitful unless you remain in Me. Yes, I Am the Vine, you're the branches. Those who remain in Me, and I in them, will produce much fruit. Apart from Me, you can do nothing. Anyone who doesn't remain in Me is thrown away like a useless branch and withers. Such branches are gathered into a pile to be burned. But, if you remain in Me and My Words remain in you, you may ask for anything you want, it will be granted!

LORD, Our Companionship is my desire above all else. Intimate communication is my heart's direction through the day. As things occur that concern me, it's You that speaks sweetly to me, 'assurance.' Your voice causes a vibration inside my heart that tells me to be aware that something is in need of deeper attention. I simply watch for what is ahead, and when I see You moving, I know to follow Your lead. This intimate conversational relationship of Ours is becoming more of a transforming habit. Step by step, moment by moment, Your Presence is my lead. You abide in me, and I in You, for You are my Savior. In Your Name Jesus Amen!

Psalm 118:24; Psalm 4:3–5; John 12:45–46

꩜

My beloved, this is the day I've made for you, Rejoice and be glad in it. You can be sure of this, I the Lord, set apart the godly for Myself. I'll answer whenever you call to Me. Don't sin by letting anger control you. Think about it over night and remain silent. Offer sacrifices in the right spirit and put your trust in Me. When you trust Me, you're not only trusting Me, but the One who sent Me. I've come as a Light to Shine in this dark world, so all who put their trust in Me will no longer remain in the dark.

LORD, I trust you! I want to see things in my life from Your view. But even when You don't provide that for me, I'm still aware You're there, and You see all, and I trust You. I want You to Choreograph my life. I surrender to Your Will and Way. Your Ways are higher than mine, and from your perspective, *'all things work together for my good.'* My desire is to live my life close to You. I'm willing to 'take risks' if they're of Your directing. The easy way is more often not the very best way, but close to You is where I'll be. I'll follow Your lead this day, for You're full of miracles, surprises, and suddenlies! How exciting to serve You today! In Jesus' Name, Amen!

I Samuel 16:7; John 8:15–16; Romans 8:38–39

~

My beloved, don't judge any by appearance or height, for I may have rejected them. I don't see things the way you see them. People judge by outward appearance, but I look at the heart. You judge Me by human standards, I do not judge anyone at all. And if I did, My judgment would be correct in every respect, because I Am not alone. You're convinced that nothing can ever separate you from My Love. Neither death or life, angels or demons, your fears for today, or your worries about tomorrow. Not even the powers of hell can separate you from My Love. No power in the sky or on the earth below can separate you from My Love that is revealed to you in My Son.

LORD, I'm grateful that my performance does not determine my value to You. I'm blessed and honored to serve You, but its not a requirement, simply a blessing. You use it to transform me, showing me your heart of Love that is in me as I give myself as an offering to You. When I'm completely surrendered in Our relationship I can be myself. You know me completely, and Your Love is unconditional. Whatever's good or bad in my life, You use to transform me. Turning all to good, for Your Glory, and for Your Good pleasure. When I'm weak You're Strong. In Your Grace I'll be strong too! I'm completely Yours my King, eternally! In Jesus' Name, Amen!

Philippians 4:6–8, 13;
Hebrews 12:12–13

❧

My child, don't worry about anything; instead, pray about everything. Tell Me what you need, and thank Me for all I've done. Then you'll experience My Peace, which exceeds anything you can understand. My Peace will guard your heart and mind as you live your life in My Son, Jesus. Now dear one, fix your thoughts on what is true, honorable, right, pure, lovely, and admirable. Think about things that are excellent and worthy of praise. You can do everything through Jesus, My Son, who gives you strength. So take a new grip with your tired hands and strengthen your weak knees. Mark out a straight path for your feet so that those who are weak and lame will not fall but become strong.

LORD, I Love to look at Your Face! It fills my soul with Peace, and Your gaze at me is overwhelming. I'll fix my eyes on You, from where my Help comes! You lift me up when all around me seems helpless and empty. You reach down in my heart and touch my faith to strengthen it. You Lord, are on my side. I'm a strong and mighty "Warrior" because of Your Presence in my life. I'll never give up Hope! I am encouraged by Your continual intervention in my life and the lives of those I see around me. You, Jesus, are absolutely in Control of all that concerns me. I smile at the future, because I know the Greatest One! You hold it all in the palm of Your Strong Hands! "I do Believe in You!" and I'll stay close to You my King, always! In Jesus' Name, Amen!

Matthew 11:28–30; Joshua 1:5,9

～

"Come to Me, all who are weary and carry heavy burdens, and I'll give you rest. Take My yoke upon you. Let Me teach you, because I am humble and gentle at heart. You'll find rest for your soul. For My yoke is easy to bear, and the burden I give you is light." No one will be able to stand against you my child, as long as you live. For I'll be with you as I was with Moses. I'll not fail you or abandon you. This is My command; "Be Strong and Courageous! Do not be afraid or discouraged. For I, the Lord your God, Am with you wherever you "Go."

LORD, I come to You, in the early morning hours, because I long to draw near to You, and to listen for Your Voice. I sit here quietly, knowing our quiet, intimate time in conversational communion will prepare me for what this day will hold. Anything that comes my way, must first be run by You for the OK! I'll not fear or worry about the things that might occur, but I'll rest and relax in the safety of Your peace-filled Presence. I'm listening for what You're teaching me today. *I'll continue trusting You completely!* I Love You my Father, deeply. In Jesus' Name, Amen!

Philippians 4:19; Psalm 75:2–3; Psalm 18:30, 34, 36

My beloved, I, the same God who takes care of you, will supply all your needs from My glorious riches, which have been given to you in Jesus My Son. At the same time I've planned, I'll bring justice against the wicked. When the earth quakes and its people live in turmoil, I Am the One who keeps its foundations firm. My Way is perfect. All My Promises prove true. I Am a Shield to all who look to Me for protection. I train your hands for battle, I strengthen your arm to draw a bronze bow. I've made a wide path for your feet to keep them from slipping.

LORD, my focus is on You today as I sit here quietly in Your Presence. I hear the birds outside singing, and I realize all of creation Worships You. That's what we were all created for. You Lord, are worthy of more than I could possibly imagine. You only ask for me, and for my time. I'll keep my heart's eyes focused on You and on Your Abundance for me today. In anticipation, I'll intimately communicate my heart to You. Listening intently for the dreams in Your heart. *Your Peace* and *Your glorious riches* are mine to enjoy, both 'Now and Forever!' In Jesus' Name, Amen!

Matthew 13:45–46; James 1:2–6a; Psalm 116:5–6

≈

"My Kingdom in heaven is like a merchant on the lookout
for choice pearls. When he discovers a pearl of great value,
he sells everything he owns and he buys it!" When troubles
come your way, consider it an opportunity for great joy. You
know that when your faith is tested, your endurance has a
chance to grow. So let it grow, for when your endurance is
fully developed, you will be perfect and complete, needing
nothing. If you need wisdom, ask Me, your generous Father,
and I'll give it to you. I'll not rebuke you for asking. But
when you ask Me, be sure that your faith is in Me alone.
How kind, good, and merciful I am to you. I, your Lord
protect those with childlike faith; you were facing death, and
I saved you.

LORD, You are my Peace. When I have concerns or feel overwhelmed, You're there for me; Your wisdom and grace in abundance for me. I only need to believe and receive your Love with a heart of thankfulness, and put my trust in You. You shed Your blood to purchase my life and to give me Peace and I receive it. I'll Praise You My Savior and Lord, all the days of my life. I'll serve you with a heart of passion in every circumstance that comes my way. I know that each day contains opportunities to please You, and that is what I live to do everyday. In Jesus' Name, Amen!

Hebrews 13:15; II Corinthians 3:17–18; Psalm 73:23–24

∽

My beloved, offer through Jesus a continual sacrifice of Praise to Me, proclaim your allegiance to My Name. Don't forget to do good and to share with those in need. These are the sacrifices that please Me. I, your Lord, Am the Spirit, and wherever My Spirit is, there is freedom. All who have had the veil removed can see and reflect My Glory. And I, your Lord, who Am the Spirit, make you more and more like Me as you are changed into My glorious image. Yet you still belong to Me, I hold your right hand. I guide you with My counsel, leading you to a glorious destiny.

LORD, I am surrounded by Your Love when I am in the stillness of Your Presence. I can lose track of time here, because my desire is to be with You. I am transformed inside and out, for I know that as I grow in intimate relationship with You, the effect is seen and felt by those around me. I want to be all that You desire me to be, no matter what it takes. I surrender my Lord, to Your Spirit and to Your will for my life. I draw closer to You with a deep longing to live a God-breathed life, trusting You'll show me Your way today step by step. I'll follow Your lead into my glorious destiny. In Jesus' Name, Amen!

John 16:33; Psalm 112:4, 7–9

∽

My beloved, My Son Jesus has told you all things so that you'll have peace in Me, God the Father. Here on earth you'll have many trials and sorrows. But take heart because through Christ Jesus My Son, I have overcome the world. Light shines in the darkness for the godly. You are generous, compassionate, and righteous. You do not fear bad news; you confidently trust in Me your Lord, to take care of you. You're confident and fearless, and you can face your foes triumphantly. Share freely and give generously to those in need. Your good deeds will always be remembered. You'll have both great influence and honor.

LORD, Your indwelling Spirit helps to show me the right path to follow and the right attitude to have while I walk it. I realize that things don't always go perfect in this life. Troubles will and do come my way but, You're here with me to deliver me from them all. You're the Perfect One, helping me to find the perfect way. I only need to keep my relationship with You close, and I'll grow in understanding and my purpose will be fulfilled in and through You. I put my trust in You my Lord, even when it's dark, You're here! My life is in Your hands, but my response to it, is in mine today. I'll stay close to Your Presence, safe, always. In Jesus' Name, Amen!

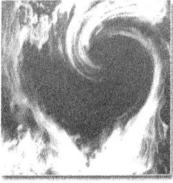

Proverbs 3:1–8

My child, never forget the things I have taught you. Store My Commands in your heart. If you do this, you'll live many years, and your life will be satisfying. Never let loyalty and kindness leave you! Tie them around your neck as a reminder. Write them deep within your heart. Then you'll find favor with Me and people, and you'll earn a good reputation. Trust Me with all your heart; don't depend on your own understanding. Seek My Will in all you do, and I'll show you which path to take. Don't be impressed with your own Wisdom. Instead, fear Me and turn away from evil. Then you'll have healing for your body and strength for your bones.

LORD, I trust in you with all of my heart. My desire is to one day, *enter heaven with You my Savior*. But first, I'll fulfill all that You've created me to do *here on earth*. I want to reach as many hearts as possible with the good-news of Your salvation. Then Lord, I know there's more transformation that must take place within me to ready me for eternity in heaven. I am willing and my heart is surrendered to You my King. *I'll lean not on my own understanding*, but in all my decisions acknowledge You, relying on You, my Shepherd and King. I press on, into Your Presence, finding, as I walk *with You* on this life-path, more of Your abundant Love and Gifts than I can imagine are available to me. Thank You Lord for Your many blessings and peace, today and always. In Jesus' Name, Amen!

Matthew 28:20;
Psalm 34:11–15, 18–19, 22

∽

Teach new disciples to obey all the commands I've given to you. Be sure that I Am with you always, even to the end of the age. Come, my child, listen to Me and I'll teach you to fear Me. Do you want to live a life that is long and prosperous? Then keep your tongue from speaking evil, and your lips from telling lies! Turn away from evil and do good. Search for peace, and work to maintain it. My eyes are watching over you who do right, my ears are open to your cries for help. I'm close to the brokenhearted; I rescue those whose spirits are crushed. Righteous people face many troubles, but I come to the rescue each time. I, the Lord will redeem you who serve Me. No one who takes refuge in Me will be condemned.

LORD, I love our continual intimate conversational relationship. I respond to it differently, depending on my circumstances, but You, Lord, are always the same. Your heart toward me never changes. Your Love is unconditional and beyond measure. You're always with me, even when I don't recognize You. *"You are there"* teaching me all things, and causing me to be transformed. You've designed my everyday events. You know just what I need, to become just what You want me to be. When You alone are my focus, the process is much easier. When I'm conscious of Your Presence, and the eyes of my heart are watching You, my opportunities are endless. I can see that You're beckoning me. Your desire for my daily life is new to me every morning. You my Lord, 'know me the best and Love me the most!' I'm blessed in You, today and always! I Love You! In Jesus' Name, Amen!

Intimacy Today: His Heart – My Heart

123

Genesis 1:27; II Corinthians 10:3–5; Isaiah 26:3

～

My beloved, I created man in My own image. I created them in My image, male and female, I created them! You are human, but don't wage war as humans do. Use My mighty weapons, not worldly weapons, to knock down the strongholds of human reasoning and to destroy false arguments. Destroy every proud obstacle that keeps people from knowing Me. Capture their rebellious thoughts and teach them to obey Me. I'll keep in perfect peace, all who trust in Me, all whose thoughts are fixed on Me. Trust Me always, for I, the Lord Am your eternal Rock.

LORD, I praise You, and with a thankful heart I realize that *I am free* to do as I will. The enemy of my soul cannot control my mind, because I can take my every thought captive. I think about You and the things that are of You, like the gifts of; Joy, Mercy, Grace, Kindness, Holiness, Thankfulness, a Good report, and so much more that are available to me because of You. Your radiant Light is mine in Your Presence and Your unconditional Love is mine forevermore. I know that *all the promises in Your Word are mine, and You guard my heart and mind today, keeping me in Your perfect Peace!* In Jesus' Name, Amen!

Psalms 116:1–2, 6–9;
Proverbs 15:24–26

~

My beloved, you Love Me because I hear your voice and your prayers for mercy. Because I bend down to 'listen,' you'll pray as long as you have breath! I protect those with child-like faith. You were facing death and I saved you. Let your soul be at rest again, for I, your Lord, have been good to you. I saved you from death, your eyes from tears, and your feet from stumbling. So walk in My Presence as you live here on earth! The path of life leads upward for the wise; they leave the grave behind. I tear down the house of the proud; but protect the property of widows. I detest evil plans; but I delight in pure words.

LORD, I surrender my life to You. My thoughts are sinful at times, with many concerns that are not my own. Thoughts of not only good, but sometimes wrong and selfish thoughts. I ask You Lord, to free me from them, and cause me to be quiet before You and not concern myself. I want to just trust You. You're aware of all that concerns me, and You have every concern of mine covered by Your shed blood. Let my thoughts be Your thoughts and my ways Your ways. I want to remember to come under submission to You, and not fear, from this day forward. Lord give me strength and wisdom to believe. In Jesus' Name, Amen!

Psalm 28:7 Matthew 6:33–34; Psalm 56:3–4; Psalm 11:8

~

My beloved, I Am your Strength and Shield! Trust Me with all your heart. I help you, and fill your heart with Joy. You burst out in songs of thanksgiving. Seek My Kingdom above all else, live righteously, and I will give you everything you need. Don't worry about tomorrow, for tomorrow will bring its own worries. Today's trouble is enough for today. When you're afraid, put your trust in Me. Praise Me for what I've promised you. If you trust in Me, why should you be afraid? What can anyone do to you? The godly are rescued from trouble, and it falls on the wicked instead.

LORD, You are my Strength and my protection. I put my trust in You alone. Your Word tells me that You will never leave me, or forsake me. I am secure in the fact that You're in complete control of all that comes my way, always. If I have any questions, I can talk with You about them, or simply watch for Your answers, and I'll see what You're intricately teaching me. Fear and worry are not as important as I think. If I give in to them, I give them my time; they can't just take it. When I trust You, fear and worry have no place in me. You, Lord, are my Great Defender, and You are Greater than anything my King! Hallelujah! In Jesus' Name, Amen!

Psalm 18:28–30; Psalm 91:11–12; II Corinthians 5:7–8

~

My beloved, I Light a Lamp before you. I, the Lord your God Light up your darkness. In My Strength you can crush an army, and with Me, you can scale a wall. My way is perfect, and all of My Promises prove true. I Am your Shield, look to Me for your protection. I'll order My Angels to protect you wherever you go. They'll hold you up with their hands so you won't even hurt your foot on a stone. For you Live by believing and not by seeing. Yes, you are fully confident, you'd rather be away from this earthly body, for then you'd be at home with Me.

LORD, I'll watch and follow You closely today as I walk out this journey that You've set before me. *This is the day that You've made, I'll 'Rejoice' and be glad in it.* Your plans and purposes for my life-path daily, are to teach me Your Ways which I desire to walk in to learn of You. I surrender my heart to Your will, and I chose to follow You in order to make a difference in this world for Your Kingdom. I say "Yes Lord, Here I am, send me!" I Love you my King, and I'll *walk by faith not by sight,* watching for Your intentions set before me all along the way. In You I'm fully confident and I'll run the race by faith because with You I'm truly alive! In Jesus' Name, Amen!

Romans 12:2; Psalm 105:4; Proverbs 14:26–27

~

My child, don't copy the behaviors and customs of this world, but let Me transform you into the new person by changing the way you think. Then you'll learn to know My Will for you, which is good and pleasing and perfect. Search for Me and for My Strength, continually seek Me. Those who fear Me are secure. I'll be a refuge for your children. The fear of Me is a Life-giving fountain; it offers escape from the snares of death. I'll remember you when I show favor to My people, I'll come near and rescue you. I'll let you share in the prosperity of My chosen ones. Rejoice in the Joy of My people, and let your Praise to Me be with those who are My heritage.

LORD, as I set my focus on You today, I am at Peace. When I'm focused on You in the quiet of the morning; my spirit is at ease and my mind cleared of all concerns. Just drawing in closer to You, for these first few moments of my day, helps me to know that You are all that I need. Even in these intimate times, Your awesome Strength is more than apparent to me. I fear nothing when I know that You are surrounding me. I'll keep the knowledge of Your Presence my primary focus throughout this day. I'll remain confident, strong, and watchful of You above all else. I rejoice in knowing that You'll show up to remind me of Your Presence in many ways, and I'll be watching for You my King! In Jesus' Name, Amen!

Romans 8:31–32;
Psalm 139:13–14, 17–18, 23–24

My child, what shall you say about such wonderful things as these? If I Am for you, who can ever be against you? Since I didn't spare even My own Son but gave Him up for you all, won't I also give you everything else? I made the delicate parts of your body and knit you together in your Mother's womb. Thank Me for making you so wonderfully complex! My workmanship is marvelous, how well you know it. How precious are My thoughts about you. They cannot be numbered! I can't even count them; they outnumber the grains of sand! When you wake up, I'll still be with you! I, your God, search and know your heart; I test you and I know your anxious thoughts. I point out to you everything in you that offends Me, with gentle nudges, and then I lead you on the path of everlasting Life!

LORD, I thank You for Your watchful eye. Nothing can touch my life that is not approved by You first. I know I can trust that You will be with me, to walk me through everything in this life. *Today is the day that You have made, and I'll rejoice and be glad in it!* Watching You unfolding before me, all that is in Your Will and plans for me, I say, 'Yes Lord,' and I surrender all in order to be Your hands extended to a lost and dying world. May Your Light and Love so shine in me that God the Father will be glorified. Then I'll be changed. I want more of You my Lord, and less of me. I Love You! In Jesus' Name, Amen!

Numbers 6:24–26;
Psalm 51:5–6, 10–13

I, your Lord bless you and protect you. I smile on you, and I'm gracious to you. I, your Lord, show you favor and I give you Peace. You were born a sinner, and yes, from the moment your Mother conceived you. But I desired honesty from the womb, teaching you wisdom even there. I created in you a clean heart. I, Your God, renewed a loyal spirit in you. I'll not banish you from My Presence, and I'll not take My Holy Spirit from you. I'll restore to you the Joy of your salvation, and I'll continually make you willing to obey Me. Then you will teach My ways to rebels, and they'll turn from their rebellion, and return to Me.

LORD, in my weakness, you alone are my Strength and my Song. Lord, You created me in my Mother's womb, in the likeness of Your image, to Worship You and to share Your amazing Love, and the Good News of Your Salvation with others. My heart is to follow Your lead, making myself available to You always. I'll not plan my own strategy, but watch for Yours. With a heart of thankfulness and complete trust in You, *I live and move and have my being.* I continue on this intimate walk with You, knowing, without a doubt, that the end result is an eternity in heaven. I walk by faith and not by sight, listening for Your voice, and grasping tightly to Your Strong right hand. I keep Going, forward!" In Jesus' Name, Amen!

Romans 8:1–2, 6–8; Psalm 46:1–2

～

*My child, there's no condemnation for you who are
surrendered to Jesus, My Son. Because you belong to Jesus,
the power of the life-giving Spirit has freed you from the
power of sin that leads to death. Your sinful nature is always
hostile toward Me. It has never obeyed My laws and never
will. That's why those who are not surrendered, and are still
under the control of their sinful nature can never please
Me. I Am your Refuge and Strength, always ready to help
in troubles. So do not be afraid when the earth shakes, and
when the mountains move and even crumble.*

LORD, I have so many unanswered questions that I know You have the
answers for, so I put my trust in You. I'm sure of the fact, that I see You in
every situation and Your outcome is always best. Your Word tells me that
You know the beginning and the end, and *all of time is in Your hands. You
redeem the time,* so I have no need to feel anxious. The things I see with my
natural eyes are not what You see from Your view. You see things through
Eyes of Truth, and not imagination. Your view is what I desire. At times
You show me Your view, but at other times You ask me to simply trust You,
and I do. In the quietness of the day You faithfully assure my heart of Your
Presence, and I find the Peace I need to *"Press in and Press On!"* In Jesus'
Name, Amen!

Ephesians 2:6–10; Proverbs 4:11–12

～

My beloved, I can point to you in all future ages an example of the incredible wealth of My Grace and Kindness toward you, as shown in all I've done for you who are surrendered to My Son, Jesus Christ. I saved you by My Grace when you believed. You cannot take credit for this; it is a Gift from Me. Salvation is not a reward for the good things you've done, so no one can boast about it. You're My masterpiece. I've created you anew in Jesus, so you can do the good things I planned for you long ago. I teach you wisdom's ways and lead you on straight paths. When you walk you won't be held back, and when you run you won't stumble.

LORD, You alone are my *Strength and Shield*. When I know You're with me, I know that *'I can do all things.'* No circumstance in this world is impossible with You. Peace is mine on this very day, because I choose to walk in the Light of Your Presence. At times I may feel myself sinking in the midst of hard things, but then I remember that *Your Word* assures me that; *"No weapon formed against me will prosper!"* I chose to 'Stand!' I'll walk in Your Light and Love, *'Ready'* at any time to do Your will, everyday! I say 'Yes!' In Jesus' Name, Amen!

Psalm 27:7–9; II Corinthians 4:7; Isaiah 12:2

∽

My beloved, I hear you as you pray, I'm merciful and I answer you! Your heart has heard Me say, 'Come here and talk with Me!' Your heart responds, 'Lord here I am, I'm coming!' I won't turn My back on you. I will not reject you, My servant, in anger. I've always been your Helper. I won't leave you or abandon you now or ever. I Am the God of your Salvation! Even if your natural parents leave you, I will hold you close to Me. You now have this Light shining in your heart, but you yourself are like a fragile jar containing this great treasure. This makes it clear that your great power is from Me, not from yourself. I've come to save you. Trust Me, and don't be afraid. I'm your Strength and Song, I've given you Victory!

YES LORD, You are my Strength and my Song! I'll worship You all the days of my life. I'm so thankful for Your tender mercies, and Your Hand of protection in my times of trouble. You're my Peace in the midst of any storm, and Your Love for me is more than amazing. I am blessed on this journey of life, because I can call You my own. I can share You with others and never feel less of You, but more. You draw me close when I'm in a time of sorrow, and You restore my Joy. You'll never leave me or forsake me. *I am truly Yours!* In Jesus' Name, Amen! 'Hallelujah!'

Psalm 32:5–8, 11

❧

Finally, My child, you confessed all your sins before Me and
stopped trying to hide your guilt. You confess your rebellion
toward Me, and I, Your Father have forgiven you. All guilt
is gone! Let all the godly come and pray to Me while there is
still time, You'll not drown in the floodwaters of judgment.
I Am your hiding place; I protect you from trouble.
I surround you with 'Songs of Victory!' I'll guide you along
the best pathway for your life. I'll advise you and watch over
you. Rejoice in me and be glad, you who obey Me. Shout for
Joy, you My beloved, whose heart is pure! The guilty walk a
crooked path, but you, My innocent travel a straight road.

LORD, I come to our quiet place, to sit in Your Presence and rest. I love
this time alone with You. These moments of Peace in Your Presence that
make all of life worth living. You show me who I am, and I find my identity
and purpose in this precious time with You. In our intimate conversational
communion, You speak to my heart, the desires of Yours, and I'm honored
to know Your Love in such a way. Yet still, there's a knowing in the depths
of me that Your dreams are mine to know, because I'm Yours. I'll read Your
Word, and find confirmation and wisdom in its pages for my day. Then I'll
go from this quiet place, to face the day with confidence of Your continual
Presence with me. I can do anything You ask of me without hesitation, because I've aligned my heart with Yours today. In Jesus' Name, Amen!

John 1:4–5; Hebrews 12:3

~

Beloved, My Word gave Life to everything that was created, and Jesus' Life gave Light to everyone. My Light shines in the darkness, and the darkness can never extinguish it. Keep your eyes on Jesus, the Champion who initiates and perfects your faith. Because of the Joy awaiting Him, Jesus endured the cross, disregarding its shame. Now My Son, is seated in the place of Honor beside Me, His Father's throne. My child, don't make light of My discipline, and don't give up when I correct you. I discipline you because I Love you, and I punish you, because I accept you as My beloved child.

LORD, I long to be aware of the Light of Your Love in every moment of the day. I watch for You in the midst of every circumstance that arises. You never fail to Shine! You can always be seen by anyone who is looking for You. You're Alive, and You're never hiding from Your surrendered children who are watching for You. My faith is alive and strengthened as I watch You, my Champion! Oh the Joy of knowing You intimately. I thank You for the Cross, I honor You, and I pray Your Love and Light will shine in and through me, my Savior, so that others will see Your good work and Your radiant reflection of Light. I desire to Glorify You through my life this day and always. Hosanna to my King! In Jesus' Name, Amen!

Hebrews 12:1, 12–13; Proverbs 27:17; Isaiah 41:13

‿

My beloved, since you're surrounded by a huge crowd of
witnesses to the life of faith, strip off every weight that slows
you down. Yes, even the sin that so easily trips you up. Run
with endurance the race that I've set before you. Take a new
grip with your tired hands and strengthen your weak knees.
Mark out a straight path before your feet so that anyone
weak and lame will not fall but will become strong too.
As iron sharpens iron, so a good friend sharpens a friend.
I, your Lord hold you up, and I say, "Do not be afraid, I Am
here to help you."

LORD, I'm "Fearlessly Surrendered" to You! I chose to walk with You boldly along this path of life You've set before me. I stand in authority coupled with Love, and I know this is just like You, my Jesus. I trust, You walk with me because You've proven it to me over and over again. I can face any problem that comes my way, because You're in me. You're in process of transforming the who I was, to the who You created me to be. I look back and see the changes in myself, and I know that You used every circumstance of my life for Your Glory. I am grateful for the changes, and through it all, I've learned to trust You all the more. *My faith is alive, and I'll* Press In and Press On toward *the high calling that is in me, holding tightly to Your Strong Right Hand!* You Lord are my Redeemer, the Holy One of Israel! In Jesus' Name, Amen!

Luke 1:37, 45–51; Psalm 57:2–3

*Nothing is impossible with Me! You, My beloved, are blessed
because you believed that I, your Savior would do what
I said. Oh, how you Praise Me, and your spirit rejoices in
Me, your God and Savior. I took notice of your lowliness
and from now on all generations will call Me blessed. I, the
Mighty One, am Holy. I've done great things for you. I show
mercy from generation to generation, to all who fear Me. My
Mighty Arm has done tremendous things! You cry out to Me
the God Most High. I'll fulfill My purpose for you. I'll send
help from heaven to rescue you, disgracing those who hound
you. I send to you My unfailing Love and Faithfulness.*

LORD, I am at rest in Your Presence. I know You're *already* aware of all that
concerns me, and You have it all planned out. You've choreographed each
moment of my day long ago, before I was born, for my transformation. You
are trustworthy and You've told me that You *'trust me.'* I'll stay in intimate
communication with You in order to know the dreams of Your heart for me.
You've shown Your mercy from generation to generation. I'll watch for You
my Redeemer, and follow hard after You. I give over my will, and I surrender
to Your Will my Savior. You my dear Shepherd, are intricately directing
my path every day, if I'm watching I will see You. In Jesus' Name, Amen!

Isaiah 30:15, 18; Psalm 62:5–8

⸻

My beloved, this is what I say; "Only in turning to Me, and resting in My Presence, will you be saved. In quietness and in confidence is your strength. You would have none of it. I your Lord, must wait for you to Come to Me so I can show you My Love and My Compassion for you. I Am your Faithful God! Blessed are you who wait for My help. Wait quietly before Me, your hope is in Me. I alone Am your Rock and your Salvation, your Fortress where you will not be shaken. Your Victory and honor come from Me alone. I Am your Refuge, a Rock where no enemy can reach you. My child, trust in Me at all times. Pour out your heart to Me for I Am your Refuge!

LORD, as I leave this morning into a long day, I realize that this time is going to be different, but I'll find times of quietness with You. In the midst of it all. I will be expecting You to provide divine appointments, opportunities that would not be there in my everyday life, unless I ask You, and I'm watching. My expectancies are different and so are my circumstances. *You my Jesus, are the same yesterday, today, and forever.* I can count on You to bring Your abundance my way. In the changes of this world around me, You Lord are the *Comforter* of my life. No matter what is different, I am safe and secure in You. I look forward to Your strategic way for my life today. In Jesus' Name, Amen!

Psalm 73:23–24, 28;
Philippians 3:13b, 20

My beloved, you still belong to Me, and I hold onto your right hand. I guide you with My counsel, and lead you to a glorious destiny. How good it is for you to be near Me. You've made Me your Sovereign Lord, and your Shelter. You'll tell everyone about the wonderful things I have done. Focus on this! Forget the past and look forward to the future and what lies ahead, live present to future. For you are a citizen of heaven where I, your Lord live. You're eagerly waiting for the return of your Savior, who takes your weak mortal body and transforms you into His glorious design. Using the same Power, He'll bring everything under His control.

LORD, when things in my life make me feel like I'm falling, I remember that You're there with me always. Your Words of promise assure me, and my experience of Your Presence daily, causes all my fears to cease. I will not dwell on the negative 'what ifs!' But I'll walk in confidence, holding securely to *Your Strong Right Hand*. Father, as You show me Yourself in the very center of my life, I'll watch for Your direction and follow Your lead. I'll stay in intimate communication with You always. For You counsel my heart with Your Love and Your Glory. My faith is continually growing and I'm becoming more fearless in my devotion to You. I wait patiently for the glorious days of heaven, not soon forgetting to *surrender to Your will for my life* this day! In Jesus' Name, Amen!

Matthew 28:19–20;
II Corinthians 5:16–19

❧

My beloved, 'Go' make disciples of all nations, baptizing them in the Name of the Father, Son, and Holy Spirit. Then teach them to obey all of My Commands. Be sure of this, "I Am with you always, even to the end of the age!" You've stopped evaluating others from a human point of view. At one time you thought of Christ merely from a human point of view. How differently you know Him now! Anyone who belongs to Christ Jesus, My Son, has become a new person. The old life is gone; a new life has begun! All this is a gift from Me, for I brought you back to Myself through Jesus. I've given you the task of reconciling the lost to Him, no longer counting their sins against them. I, your Father, gave you this powerful, and wonderful message of reconciliation.

LORD, I Worship You alone, because of who You are! You continually challenge me in order to change me. I do not fear change. I know that you're transforming me into the likeness of Your image, and Lord, I am secure in You. I'll stick close to You with this strong desire to be all that You want me to be. Everyday You take me on new and exciting adventures, so that I'll be ready to share your awesome message of salvation and life along the way. When things are different, or difficult, I chose to be fearless and to surrender to You! I believe that this day is the day that You've made for me and I'll rejoice and be happy in it! You created me to Worship You and to share Your story with others, making disciples of many for Your Glory! In Jesus' Name, Amen!

II Corinthians 5:20–21;
Psalm 45:3, 6–7, 17

You my beloved are My ambassadors; I make My appeal through you. You speak for Jesus when you say, "Come back to God!" I made Christ Jesus, who never sinned, to be the Offering for your sins, so that you could be made right with Me. Put on your sword, mighty warrior, you're glorious and majestic! My Throne endures forever! I rule with a scepter of justice. I love justice and hate evil. I, your God, have anointed you, pouring out the oil of Joy on you more than anyone. You will bring honor to My Name in every generation. The nations will Praise Me forever and ever.

LORD, I will remember who I am, *in You*! In the midst of adverse circumstances, I'll respond with all my heart and all that I am, *in You*. You'll be glorified through me. My prayer needs are simple and humble in comparison to *Who You Are*. Your Power and Glory are mine, as I remain Joy-filled and alive with trust and hope *in You*. I rely on Your Strength and the Power of Your Holy Spirit which enables me. This causes me to *walk by faith and not by sight*. This day and eternally, I'll walk with You, my Savior and Lord, in humble yet 'fearless confidence!' I'll practice reaching generations with Your Love, and Joyfully bringing honor to Your Name. In Jesus' Name, Amen!

Colossians 2:6–7; Colossians 3:16–17; Colossians 4:5–6

~

My child, just as you've accepted My Son Jesus, as your Lord, you must continue to follow Him. Let your roots grow down into Him, and let your life be built on Him alone. Then your faith will grow strong in the truth you were taught, and you'll overflow with thankfulness. Now, let all the richness of My Son's message, fill your life. Teach and counsel others with all the wisdom I give you. Sing psalms, hymns, and spiritual songs to Me, with a thankful heart. Whatever you do or say, do as a representative of Jesus, giving thanks through Him to Me, your Father. Live wisely among those who are not believers, and make the most of every opportunity. Let your conversation be gracious and attractive so you'll have the right response for everyone.

LORD, I sit in the quietness of the morning, looking forward to the day ahead. The deepness of our intimate relationship, of continual conversation and Love, is growing stronger every day. I find that, as I spend more time in our secret place within the depths of my heart with You, I become more and more aware of the awesomeness of knowing You. Your Peace is truly mine at all times. There's a great and powerful richness to be discovered in You at moment by moment intervals, if I focus on Your Presence all around and within me. Jesus, You are my ever-present Prince of Peace, with the Peace that passes all understanding. This Peace is available to me as I need it. I will share this same Peace with those You place around me today! In Jesus' Name, Amen!

I Thessalonians 5:16–24; John 16:24

❧

Always be Joyful! Never stop praying! Be thankful in every circumstance, for this is My will for you who belong to My Son, Jesus. Don't stifle My Holy Spirit. Don't scoff at prophecies, but test everything that's said. Hold on to what's good and stay away from every kind of evil. My Peace makes you holy in every way, and I keep your spirit, soul, and body, blameless until Jesus comes again! I, your God will make this happen, for I, the One who calls you, Am faithful. You haven't done this before, Ask, using My Son's Name and you'll receive, and you'll have abundance of Joy!

LORD, our intimate conversational relationship is where I long to stay. Remaining aware of You and Your sweet Presence at all times is my greatest goal. When I allow uneasy, or empty thoughts to come in and rob me of my time with You, I feel separated from the place of Peace and safety of Your Presence. That's when I stop myself, breathe, and I take captive my thoughts, drawing close to You again. This place is by different means at all different times like singing, or humming a song of worship to You, or when I pick up Your Word focusing on its Life-giving Peace for my need. Always for me, the very best thing is simply to 'Listen for Your Voice of assurance' which fills my soul with abundance. My spirit rises up within me, and I know just who I am in You today. In Jesus' Name, Amen!

Psalm 89:14–17; Hebrews 12:14–15

My beloved, righteousness and justice are the foundation of My Throne. Unfailing Love and truth walk before Me as attendants. Happy are you who hear the joyful call to worship, for you'll walk in the Light of My Presence. You'll walk all day long in My Wonderful representation. You'll exult Me in My Righteousness, for My Names sake. I Am your Glorious Strength, and it pleases Me to make you strong. Work at living in peace with everyone, and work at living a holy life, for those who are not holy will not see Me. Look after each other so none of you fail to receive My Grace. Watch out that no bitterness grows up to trouble you, or to corrupt others also.

LORD, I sometimes feel, discouraged about things in life that affect those I love. Then I decide not to go there, not to think on those things, just distance myself, placing my heart of trust in You. I want to know You in a much deeper way, more and more every day. I thank You my Savior, I Praise You for who You are and for who You intend me to be. I'll Live in the Light of Your Presence, *'Pressing in and Pressing On'* for Your Glory. *I'll never give up!* But I'll *'Run the Race'* to the finish with my eyes focused on You. You're the One who has paved the way with Your Light and Love, and I'll follow You closely, today. In Jesus' Name, Amen!

I Corinthians 13:11–13;
Ephesians 3:16–17

My beloved, when you were a child, you spoke and thought and reasoned like a child. But, when you grew up, you put away childish things. Now you see things imperfectly as in a cloudy mirror, but soon you'll see everything with perfect clarity. All you know now is partial and incomplete, but then, you'll know everything completely, just as I, your God know you completely. Three things will last forever, Faith, Hope, and Love, and the greatest of these is Love! Pray that from My glorious unlimited resources I'll empower you with inner strength through My Spirit. Christ, My Son, will make His home in your heart as you trust Him. Your roots will grow down deep in My Love and My Love will keep you strong.

LORD, I sit in still silence this day in order to hear You within the depths of my heart. Your communication of Love is what I long for every day. I'll practice the concept of no limitations until I have it straight in my thoughts and my heart. You Lord, are always there to express Your amazing Love and fill me with more. I want to experience the fullness of Your life in me today and always. It is overwhelming, but the desire of my heart. I long for eternity with You, but I'll wait patiently because I realize that I'm in need of the transforming You provide for me here. The knowledge of Your Love for me, and Your Presence sustains me now, this day! Hallelujah! In Jesus' Name, Amen!

Colossians 4:2–4;
I Thessalonians 5:16–22

~

My child, devote yourself to intimate conversational communion with an alert and focused mind, and a thankful heart. Pray for others, this will give you many opportunities to speak about My mysterious plan concerning Christ, My Son. This is why you're here, in chains. Pray that you'll proclaim this message as clearly as you should. Always be joyful! Never stop talking with Me! Be thankful in all the circumstances of life, for this is My will for you who belong to Jesus Christ, My Son. Don't quench the Holy Spirit, or make light of prophecies, but test everything that is said. Hold on to what is good and true. Stay away from every kind of evil.

LORD, I'm at rest in Your Presence, knowing that You alone are in control of all that concerns me, and all my day holds. I don't need to rush, but simply enjoy Your walk of purpose for Me. You're the One who choreographs my life. I can trust that the time of thankfulness that overflows from the depths of my heart is as I imagine eternity with You will be. *I trust You my Lord, with all of my heart, leaning not on my own understanding, but in all my ways, I acknowledge You, and You make my path completely straight. Not my will Lord, but yours be done* in and through me today! In Jesus' Name, Amen!

Deuteronomy 29:29;
Deuteronomy 30:19–20; Psalm 32:8

❧

I, your Lord and God have secrets known to no one. You're not accountable to them, but you and your children are accountable forever to all that I've revealed to you, so that you may obey all the terms of these instructions in My Word. Today, I give you the choice between life and death, between blessings and curses. Now, I call on heaven and earth to witness your choice. Oh my child, choose Life, then you and your descendants might Live! You can make this choice by Loving Me, obeying Me, and also by continually committing yourself firmly to Me. This is the Key to your Life! If you love and obey Me, you'll live long in the land I have given you and I swore to your ancestors, generation to generation, Abraham, Isaac, and Jacob! I Am Your Shepherd and Guide.

LORD, I reach out and hold tightly to Your hand, trusting and surrendering to You Jesus, my Savior, my King. Guide me this day by Your Spirit, as I listen to Your gentle voice of passion and truth prompting my hearts direction. What my future holds is within Your faith-filled hands, and as I look ahead, heaven to earth, to Your miraculous, outrageous outcome that You've told me of, and that only You can provide. No matter what the day brings, as long as You're there. I'll stay focused on You. I can do all things because You are my Strength and my Joy. In Your Presence my Joy is made full even in my weakness. I'll stay in Your Presence, step by step, in obedience to Your will, one day at a time. In Jesus' Name, Amen!

Psalm 73:23; I Corinthians 10:23–24; Psalm 37:30–31, 39–40

~

My beloved, you belong to Me! I hold you by your right hand. I guide you with My counsel, leading you to a glorious destiny. You're allowed to do anything but not everything is good for you, or beneficial. Don't be concerned for your own good but for the good of others. My godly one, offer good counsel; teach right from wrong. You've made My Law's your own so you will not slip from My path. I rescue the godly. I Am your fortress in times of trouble. I, your Lord, help you, I rescue you from the wicked. I save you, and you find your shelter in Me.

LORD, my eyes are directed toward You, my Savior. You alone are where my help comes from. When burdens come my way, I'll not forget that You are with me, and I'll not lose sight of Your protective strength. Your Spirit is always reminding me of Your Presence and I'm fully aware that You will not allow me to fail. Worrying has become a distant memory because I am learning to put my trust and hope in You My King. My burdens are lighter because of Your great Love and assurance within me. You Lord, make my path straight. I'll watch and follow You close today. In Jesus' Name, Amen!

Philippians 4:4–7, 13; Isaiah 26:3–4

My beloved, always be full of Joy in Me. I say it again— Rejoice! Let everyone see that you're considerate in all you do. Remember, I your Lord, Am coming soon! Don't worry abut anything; pray about everything. Tell Me what you need, and thank Me for all I've done. Then you'll experience My Peace, which far exceeds anything you can understand. My Peace will guard your heart and mind as you live your life in Me. You can do everything through Me, I give you My Strength. I'll keep you in perfect Peace, you who trust in Me, all whose thoughts are fixed on Me. Trust Me always, for I the Lord God, Am your Eternal Rock!

MY LORD, I come to You this day, to our private place that I Love best. the quietness and Peace within Your Presence. I bring to You my Savior, my heart, filled with thanksgiving for only You. You've carried me through everything. You've proven to me again, that You are there for me always, and You are able to keep me in perfect Peace! I have learned to trust You my Lord, and I'm excited about the place I find myself now. *Trusting You is a habit I'm to practice continually.* As we have intimate communion today, I'll worship You, and I'll praise Your Name, from the very depths of my heart with thankfulness. And I trust that You'll fill me with Your Peace today. In Jesus' Name, Amen!

John 11:25; Matthew 11:28–30; I Peter 1:8–9

～

I Am the Resurrection and Life! Believe in Me and Live, even after dying. Everyone who lives in Me and believes in Me will never die. Believe this! "Come to Me, if your weary and carry heavy burdens, and I'll give you rest. Take My yoke upon you. Let Me teach you, I Am humble and gentle of heart. In Me, you'll find rest for your soul. My yoke is easy to bear, and the burden I give you is light." Love Me, even though you've never seen Me. Though you don't see Me now, trust Me; and you'll rejoice with a glorious, inexpressible Joy. Your reward for trusting Me, is the Salvation of your soul.

LORD, as this morning is moving forward into the day, I sit in the quietness of what is left of it, in the comfort of Your Presence. This is the place of pleasure that I can come to daily, from moment to moment. Time is moving on, aging is happening to this earthly body now, whether I like it or not, but Your plans and purposes never change. You have no concern about aging because You have given me abundant life. I'm filled with You, and I can do all things because You strengthen me. Your Joy and Glory are mine in Your plan for me today! I am blessed both now and forever. I Love and trust You! Lord, I know Your Salvation is my great reward. Hallelujah! In Jesus' Name, Amen!

Ephesians 4:2–7; John 10:4

*My servant ambassador, always be humble and gentle.
Be patient with others, make allowances for their faults
because of your Love. Make every effort to keep unity in
the Spirit, binding yourself together with Peace. For there is
one body, and one Spirit, just as you've been called to one
glorious hope for the future. There is one Lord, one faith,
one baptism, and One God and Father. I Am over all, in
all, and living through all. I've given each one a special gift,
through the generosity of Jesus, My Son. After I gather you,
My Own flock, I'll walk ahead of you, and you'll follow Me
because you know My voice.*

LORD, this is the day You have made, and I am rejoicing in it. I'll listen today for Your voice of direction as I live my life in Love with You. I'll be ever so blessed and honored to follow You and to reach out to those who are in need of You. Your closeness and companionship are the Joy of my day, and I long to share You with others. When interrupting voices arise, I ask You for wisdom and discernment to know the difference of the Sound of You. I want to use wise words when I'm sharing You, and Your timing is important. Lord, You're the redeemer of time, and You know all things. I rely on Your wisdom leading me, and Your knowledge from beginning to end. Teach me Lord, to follow You as You're making changes in me continually. I'm learning to flow with You and enjoy it! In Jesus' Name, Amen!

I Thessalonians 5:6–13

My beloved, be on guard, not asleep like some. Stay alert and be clear-headed. Night is the time when some sleep, and drinkers get drunk. But you, who Live in the Light, be clear-headed, You're protected by the armor of Faith and Love worn as your helmet, the confidence of your salvation. I choose to save you my child, through Jesus, not to pour out My anger on you. Jesus died for you, so whether you're dead or alive when He returns, you'll Live with Him forever. Encourage others and build them up, just as you're already doing. Honor your leaders in My work, for they work hard and give you spiritual guidance. Show them great respect and deep love, because of their work. And live Peacefully with everyone.

LORD, as this day begins, I'm in awe of the opportunity to sit in quietness and intimacy with You. As we communicate heart to Heart, all that I'm concerned about seems to lose its intensity. It actually decreases to needless worry, and becomes from Your view no less than opportunities for transformation. Your participation changes the whole concept of this life. I'm aware of Your Presence in the most unlikely of places and times. I'll encourage others in You Lord today. I'll honor those who are my leaders, in some way I want to show them with expressions of thankfulness and Love. Again, I realize *that all things will work together for good for me because I am called by You, for Your purposes.* Living closer to You today than yesterday is my desire. I know by the leading of Your Spirit, I'll succeed! In Jesus' Name, Amen!

Hebrews 7:22, 25–26; Psalm 37:3

∽

*My beloved, Jesus is the One who guarantees your covenant
with Me. He's able once and forever, to save you who come
to Me through Him. He Lives, forever to intercede with
Me on your behalf. He is the kind of High Priest you need
because He alone is Holy and blameless, unstained by sin.
He's been set apart from sinners and has been given the
highest place of honor in Heaven. Trust in Me, and do good,
then you'll live safe in the land and prosper. Take delight in
Me, and I'll give you your heart's desire. Commit everything
you do to Me, Trust Me, and I'll help you. I'll make your
innocence radiant, like the noonday sun.*

LORD, I enjoy Your Presence and the closeness of my walk with You. Your
Spirit surrounds me with the sweetness of Your Love. It is here that I find
the Peace that only You can give. I draw in closer to You, and hold tight to
Your hand. I'm learning to trust You completely with my whole heart, for
this is my great desire. I'll never let go of You, my Savior. I'll Press in, and
Press on, committing everything I am. All I do is for You, and for Your Glory.
I pray I'll be a reflection of Your Peacefulness, abundant Light and radiant
Love today. You, Lord, are my High Priest, my Shepherd, and my King. *In
Your matchless Name 'Jesus' Amen!*

James 1:5, 12–18

❧

If you need wisdom ask Me, your Generous Father, and
I'll give it to you. I'll not rebuke you for asking Me. I'll
bless you who patiently endure testing and temptation.
Afterward you'll receive the crown of life that I've promised
to you who love Me. Remember when you're being tempted
not to say; God is tempting Me! I, your God never tempt you
or anyone to do wrong. Temptation comes from your own
desires, which entice you and drag you away. These wrong
desires give birth to sinful actions. When sin's allowed to
grow, it gives birth to death. Don't be mislead! Whatever is
good and perfect comes down to you from Me, your God,
who created all of the lights in the heavens. I never change
or ever cast a shifting shadow. I choose to give birth to you
by giving you My True Word, Jesus Christ. You, out of all
my creation, became My prized possession.

LORD, I Praise You for the Gift of my Jesus, Your Word. I also Praise You for these challenges that are mine this day. I know that You're with me and You've sent me Your Holy Spirit to teach me. You'll make a way when there seems to be no way. The trials, temptations, and challenges that I face, are not mine alone but ours, Yours Lord, and mine. You're teaching me to watch for You along the way, so I can learn of You, and follow. You said You would not give me more than I can handle, and that I could trust You to make a way of escape for me every time, and I can handle it. I'll consider all these various trials pure Joy—gifts from You to transform me into the likeness of Your Image. I'll rely on, trust in, and cling to You today and always, because You Lord, are my Father, the One True God. In Jesus' Name, Amen!

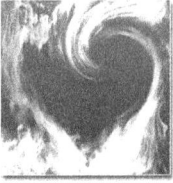

I Chronicles 16:8–12;
Matthew 6:32–b–34

My child, give thanks to Me your Lord, and proclaim My Greatness. Let the whole world know what I've done. Sing to Me, Yes, sing My Praises. Tell everyone of My marvelous deeds. Exult My Holy Name, and Rejoice, you who Worship Me. Search for Me, and for My Strength, continually seek Me. Remember the wonders I've performed, My miracles, and the rulings I've given. I, your heavenly Father already know all your needs. Seek Me and seek My Kingdom above all else, live righteously, and I'll give you everything you need. Don't worry about tomorrow, for tomorrow will bring its own worries. Today's trouble is enough for today.

LORD, I'll keep my heart in tune with Yours, as I walk the path of life today. Our intimate communication begins this morning, and it will continue throughout the day. This is my heart's desire, I want to know You more. As we walk and talk together, Your voice and Your desires become more a part of my own DNA. I find I'm learning what Your desires are, as I spend time in Your Presence. *Then I find my ways become Your ways and my thoughts Your thoughts.* We're one in the Spirit, *as You and the Father are One*, just as You said it would be. It's a gradual process. I'm being transformed while I'm spending more time with You. Lord, You're renewing my mind. In Jesus' Name, Amen!

Galatians 5:22–26; I John 4:10–12

❧

*My beloved, My Holy Spirit produces in you this kind
of fruit in your life: Love, Joy, Peace, Patience, Kindness,
Goodness, Faithfulness, Gentleness, and Self-control. There
is no law against these things! Those who belong to Jesus,
have nailed the passions and desires of their sinful nature
to His Cross and crucified them there. Since you are now
living by the Spirit, follow the Spirit's leading in every part
of your life. Do not become conceited, or provoke others,
and don't be jealous of others. Now this is real Love, not
that you loved Me, but that I Loved you and sent My Son as
a sacrifice to take away your sins. Dear one, I Loved you so
much, you surely ought to love others. No one has ever seen
Me. But if you love others, I, your God, live in you, and My
Love is brought to full expression in you.*

FATHER, as I sit here in the quietness of my own home, You're the Center
of my thoughts and heart. I'm resting and calm within, looking forward to
Your plan for 'our time' together. Time in Your Presence is soothing, and it
thrills me just to know that You're aware of all my weaknesses and You cover
them all. Fill me up Lord, with Your Light and Your Love to overflowing.
Then, I'll be for others what You intend me to be, *no more and no less,* just
You exalted above all else. *Let Your Light so shine, expressed* through me, *as
I live and move and have my being* in the Center of Your Presence. You'll be
illuminated in and through me today. In Jesus' Name, Amen!

Galatians 6:4–10

My beloved child, pay careful attention to your own work, for then you'll get the satisfaction of a job well done, and you won't need to compare yourself to anyone else. You're responsible only for your own conduct. You've been taught My Word, now you should provide for your teachers, sharing all the good things with them. Don't be mislead, you cannot mock My justice. You'll always harvest what you plant. If you live only to satisfy your own sinful nature you'll harvest decay and death from that sinful nature. If you live to please the Spirit you'll harvest everlasting life from the Spirit. So don't get tired of doing what is good. At just the right time you'll reap a harvest of blessing if you don't give up. Whenever you have the opportunity, do good to everyone, especially those in the family of faith.

FATHER, this is the day that You've made, I choose to rejoice and be glad in it, trust You for the day, moment by moment. Step by step, all that this day holds for my life You've planned for my good and not for evil. I'll walk with You through this day, looking for Your fingerprints and hand around me. Lord, I know what You supply in today is all that is needed for the transformation of my heart. I say Yes! Yes Lord, Yes to Your will and Yes, to Your ways! I'll keep on watching for opportunities, assignments prepared by You for Your Glory from the beginning. I'll keep remembering You and I'll never give up for the sake of the Cross of my Lord and Savior Jesus Christ. All Praise from my lips will be Yours forever and ever, Hallelujah! In Jesus' Name, Amen!

II Corinthians 5:7; Galatians 6:14–18

~

*My beloved, you should live by believing and not by seeing.
As for you, never boast about anything except the Cross of
your Lord, Jesus Christ. Because of the Cross, your interest in
this world has been crucified, and the world's interest in you
has died. It doesn't matter whether you've been crucified or
not. What counts is whether you've been transformed into a
new creation. My Peace and Mercy will be upon all who live
by this principle. You're My new people! From now on, don't
let anyone trouble you with these things. For you bear on
your body the scars that show you belong to Jesus Christ, My
Son. Now His Grace is with you!*

FATHER, walking by faith and not by sight is the most peaceful way to
live this life. Faith in You and Your Spirit's Power, in my life is both exciting
and fulfilling. You've shown me Your desire to empower me, to challenge my
days with assignments from You, that cause me to walk close by Your side in
continual communion with You. This is where You want me to live. I know
You want me to accomplish Your purpose and planned destiny in my life,
and the lives of those that You cause me to affect along the way. Thank You
Lord, for making my life an instrument of Your true Peace. It is a life made
limitless because of Your Son Jesus, teaching and comforting me through
Your Gifts, which You've given to me by the power of Your Holy Spirit. In
Jesus' Name, Amen!

John 14:1–4; Psalm 27:14; Hebrews 6:18–20

~

My beloved, don't let your heart be troubled, Trust your God, and trust also in Me, Jesus. There is more than enough room in My Father's house. If this were not so, would I have told you that I'm going to prepare a place for you? When everything is ready, I'll come for you, so that you'll always be with Me where I am. And you know the way to where I am going. Wait patiently for Me, your Lord. Be brave and courageous. Yes, wait patiently for Me. I've given both My Promise and My Oath. These two things are unchangeable because it is impossible for Me to lie. You, who have run to Me for refuge can have great confidence as you hold to the hope that lies before you. This hope is a strong and trustworthy anchor for your soul. It leads you through the curtain into My inner Sanctuary. Jesus went in before you. He has become your eternal High Priest in My order.

FATHER, "I trust You!" I am awed by You, over and over again as I walk through my day. I find You ribboning Yourself through it, intricately. If I'm watching, I'll be able to see You, directing my path and showing me opportunities to represent You in the lives of others continually. You're molding and shaping me within, as I stay in the atmosphere of Your Presence snuggled close and holding Your Strong hand. My hope is in You alone Lord. My intimate conversations with You cause me to be more aware of Your deep Loving desires and Your dreams for my life, and for the lives of others I may or may not know, yet. These new connections are waiting to be formed by Your own spiritual gifts, and it's our work together, Yours and mine, that bring about Your ultimate plan completely. Alignment with You, is my very own responsibility and I chose to be aligned with You, always. In Jesus' Name, Amen!

John 16:9–14; John 16:22–24

~

My beloved, the world's sin is that it refuses to believe in Me. Righteousness is available to you, because I, Jesus, have gone to our Father, and you'll not see Me anymore. Judgment comes, because the ruler of this world has already been judged. "There's so much more I want to tell you, but you can't bear it now. When the Holy Spirit of truth comes, he will guide you to all truth. He'll not speak on His own, but will tell you what He's heard. He'll tell you about the future. He'll bring Glory to Me by telling you what He receives from Me. You'll have sorrow now, but I will see you again, then you'll rejoice, and no one can rob you of that Joy! At that time, you won't need to ask Me for anything. Truthfully, you'll ask our Father directly and He'll give it to you, because you ask in My Name. You've not done this before. Ask, using My Name, and you'll receive and have Abundant Joy and Life!

LORD, what Peace Your Presence brings, no matter what the circumstances may be. This world has it's own problems and wars, natural and supernatural, but *You, My Savior, have overcome the world.* You've already caused me to be 'the winner,' I only need to receive, and walk in it. You have given me authority to walk all over my enemy in the place of victory in You. Your Presence is my staying place, where my victory resides. In You, ALL things are possible for me. As I sit with You today conversing about us, I quietly receive from You more Joy, more Peace, and all that I need to 'be an overcomer in this life. I can rest in the place of victory, even when my eyes cannot see the victory yet! Victory is here! It's visible from Your view, I can see it now, and receive it today! In Jesus' Name, Amen!

Intimacy Today: His Heart – My Heart

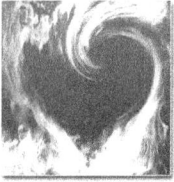

II Corinthians 3:16–18;
Ephesians 3:17–19; Psalm 46:10

∾

My beloved, whenever someone turns to Me, surrendered, the veil is taken away. For I Am the Spirit, and wherever My Spirit is, there is freedom. All who've had that veil removed can see, and reflect with radiance, My Glory. I, your Lord, Am Spirit; I make you more like Me as you are being changed into My own glorious image. I, Christ Jesus, make My home in your heart as you trust Me. Your roots grow down deep in our Father's Love and keep you strong. You have the power to understand, as all My people should, how wide, how high, and how deep My Love is. You experience My Love, though it is too great to understand fully. Then you'll be complete, with all fullness of Life and Power that comes from Father God.

FATHER, my intimate time in Your Presence is free, and yet through my life I've hesitated to be there, freely. At times I've felt that it should cost me something or be difficult to embrace. When with the veil, I always thought it would be difficult. I know now that You long for me to spend time with you, even more than I long for Your time and attention. I need You, and I think You need me. Like most things in life, the things of You, the ways of heaven are opposite of this world. I've learned to trust You, to receive from You, and to believe. In my time with You, I receive all I need from You, and my way of thinking is changed in Your Presence. Heaven to earth is my new thought process. Your view and Your ways are amazing and much so more available to me than ever I would have known. So now I sit still in Your Presence, knowing, You're my God! In Jesus' Name, Amen!

Intimacy Today: His Heart – My Heart

Philippians 4:8–9, 13;
Psalm 140:12–13; Proverbs 17:22

Now My beloved, one more thing. Fix your thoughts on what is true, and honorable, right, and pure, lovely, and admirable. Think about things that are excellent and worthy of praise. Keep putting into practice all that you've learned and received from Me. Do everything you heard from Me and saw Me doing. Then I, the God of Peace will be with you. For you can do everything through Jesus, My Son, who gives you strength. You know that I will help those persecuted. I'll give justice to the poor. Surely righteous people are Praising My Name, and the godly will Live in My Presence. A cheerful heart is good medicine, but a broken spirit saps a person's strength.

FATHER, I surrender to You. To You, to Your will, and to Your way. Your thoughts are higher than mine, and I believe You! I'm depending completely on You continually, for my every need. When I'm weak, You're my Strength, and I rejoice in relying on You my Lord. Enjoying the life You have already planned for me, makes my life so much easier than constantly trying to figure things out. I'll watch You, listen for Your still small voice of instructive grace and mercy. Then I'll whisper back to You my heart of worship all throughout the day. I sometimes find myself humming the melody of Your heart, and I realize this connection is my focus. I'll serve You today, my Lord, in Your perfect Peace and contentment. In Jesus' Name, Amen!

Psalm 139:1–8;
II Corinthians 1:21–22; Joshua 1:5

❧

I, your Lord have examined your heart and I know
everything about you. I know when you sit down, and when
you stand up. I know your thoughts even when you're far
away. I see you when you travel and when you are at rest
at home. I know everything you do. I know what you're
going to say even before you say it. I walk before you and
I follow you. I place My hand of Blessing on your head.
Such knowledge is too wonderful and too great for you
to understand. You can never escape My Spirit! You can
never get away from My Presence! It is I, your God, who
enables you to stand firm. I've commissioned you and I've
identified you as My own by placing in your heart, the Holy
Spirit as the first installment that guarantees everything I've
promised you. No one will be able to stand against you as
long as you live. I'll be with you as I was with Moses. I'll
not fail or abandon you.

LORD, as I draw close to you in the quietness of the morning, I am so
grateful for Your Love and understanding. You help me to see myself
through your Grace-filled eyes so that I don't judge myself so harshly. You
have caused me to look deeper into my own heart to see what You see there.
Truly, I've surrendered my life to You, and You are pleased; I feel it. That's
my desire, to always please You. When You decide to expose to me a part
of my heart that needs more of You, there is no condemnation in it—just
Your forgiveness and the way to escape its hold. This process causes me to
look at others from Your view in order to example Your heart of Love and

forgiveness that continually overflows and ribbons throughout our lives. You're connecting us all to You, and causing us to sing Your praises with thankfulness to You eternally. In Jesus' Name, Amen!

Psalm 84–10–12; Matthew 6:33–34

∾

My beloved, a single day in My courts is better than a thousand anywhere else! You'd rather be a gatekeeper in My house than live the 'good life' in the homes of the wicked. For I, your Lord God, Am your Sun and your Shield. I'll give you Grace and Glory. I'll withhold no good thing from you who do what is right. What Joy for those who put their trust in Me, the Lord of Heaven's Army. Seek My Kingdom, above all else, live righteously, and I'll give you everything you need. Don't worry about what tomorrow may bring. Tomorrow has its own worries. Today's trouble is enough for today.

FATHER, trusting You in ALL things, and watching for You in every area of my life, is my desire. Just when I think I have it all down pat, some unforeseen circumstance arises that causes me to worry and play out in my own mind all the possible outcomes. But, I'm learning to stop in the midst of those times, taking captive my thoughts. I'll check my own heart, and draw closer to You, for Your view. Then I'll have Your understanding of the situation. I'm aware of Your Presence, watching for You ribboning Yourself around me, this is what helps me most. Then, I remember what You've already said to me today as I read Your Word, or in our quiet moments this morning. Blanket me with more of You and less of me. I yield my life to You. And You prompt me by the gentle nudges and whispered words that come from You my Savior today. In Jesus' Name, Amen!

Romans 8:1–2; I Corinthians 6:18–20; Proverbs 21:3

⌒

My child, there is no condemnation for those who belong to Me. Because you belong to Me, the power of My life-giving Spirit has freed you from the power of sin that leads to death. Run from sexual sin! No other sin so clearly has an effect on the body as this one does. Sexual immorality is a sin against your own body. Don't you realize that your body is the temple of the Holy Spirit, who lives in you and was given to you by Me? You do not belong to yourself, for I bought you with a high price. So you must honor Me with your body. I Am more pleased with you when you do what is right and just, than when you offer Me sacrifices.

LORD, my prayer is that of Your own Words; *Let Your Light so Shine in me* that others might see Your good works and Glorify our Father in Heaven. Let me then also be *transformed by the renewing of my mind*, that I would begin to think more clearly from your view, heaven to earth. I chose to be holy as You, my Lord, are Holy, not responding in my earthly selfish way, but first, thinking from Your perspective, being quick to listen and slow to speak my response. I want You to Live in me, my Lord, inhabiting all of my thoughts, words, deeds, and emotions this day! Thank You for Your Spirit that leads me. I Love You! In Jesus Name, Amen!

Luke 11:23, 28, 34–36;
Psalm 50:14–15, 23

꩜

My child, anyone who isn't with Me opposes Me, and anyone who isn't working with Me is actually working against Me. Even more blessed are those who hear My Word and put it into practice. Your eye is a lamp that provides light for your body. When your eye is good, your whole body is filled with light. But, when it is bad, your body is filled with darkness. Make sure that the light you think you have is not actually darkness. If you're filled with light, with no dark corners, then your whole life will be radiant, as though a floodlight were filling you with light. Make thankfulness your sacrifice to Me, and keep the vows you made to your Most High. Call on Me when you're in trouble and I'll rescue you, and you will give Me the Glory! Giving thanks is a sacrifice that truly honors Me. If you keep to My path, I'll reveal to you My Salvation!

FATHER, I thank you for the outpouring of your Holy Spirit into my life. You've made my daily walk in You, a symphony of Love. I thank You, for the continual confirmation, and all the things You show me day to day. I find as time goes by, and I stick close to You, in intimate conversational relationship. You prove Yourself and Your Love for me over and over again. Lord, this causes my faith to soar and my innermost being becomes more heaven-to-earth powered today than yesterday. I'll align myself heart and soul in spirit and in truth, with You. In Your Word I'll search and grasp hold of the truths of Your faithfulness even deeper, until nothing can preoccupy my mind. In You I find all that I need to walk the life-path for You this very day. In Jesus' Name, Amen!

Psalm 95:1–7; Psalm 9:9–10; Psalm 139:23

~

Come, sing to Me, your Lord! Shout joyfully to the rock of your Salvation. Come to Me with thanksgiving. Sing psalms of Praise to Me. For I, the Lord, Am a Great God, a Great King above all gods. I hold in My hand the depths of the earth and the mightiest mountains. The sea belongs to Me for I made it. My hands formed the dry land, too. I, the Lord, Am a Shelter for the oppressed, a Refuge in times of trouble. Those who know My Name trust in Me, for I do not abandon those who search for Me. I search for you and know your heart, I test you and know your anxious thoughts.

LORD, I rejoice in You and I am oh so glad, as I thank You this day for all that You're doing and have done in my life. My thankful heart sings as I think of all the ways You've touched me, and brought an awareness of Your Presence and Your direction into me. Trusting You has become a more natural reaction, instead of fear these days. I find that Your Peace is mine continually, when I have a trusting and grateful heart present within me. You my Lord, have changed me and brought a greater revelation of Yourself to me these days. I walk with an assurance of You, and me. I walk in a new authority coupled with love that looks just like You my King; with a Sure and a Peaceful Trust in You today! In Jesus' Name, Amen!

Luke 8:16–18; Psalm 119:65–67

My beloved, no one lights a lamp and then covers it with a bowl or hides it under a bed. A lamp is placed on a stand, where its light can be seen by all who enter the house. For all that is in secret will eventually be brought into the open. Everything that's concealed will be brought to light and be made known to all. Pay attention to how you hear. To those who listen to My teaching, more understanding will be given. Those who are not listening, even what they think they understand will be taken away from them. I've done many good things just as I promised. Believe in My commands, and teach good judgment and knowledge. You used to wander off until I disciplined you, but now you closely follow My Words.

LORD, I am overflowing in abundance with You, my Lord. Our intimacy in the quietness of the morning, and throughout the day, seems to be continually growing. Conversations with You have become more frequent, and often, my desire is to be continually in them. I know that because of who You are, I'm becoming, in You, who You originally designed me to be. Transform me Lord! I long to become an even greater blessing to You, as Your child. You shower me with Your own heart's delight, and Your abundance is mine today and always. I love You my Jesus, In Your Name, Amen!

Hebrews 13:2–8

❧

Don't forget to show hospitality to strangers, for some
who've done this have entertained angels without realizing
it! Remember those in prison, as if you were there yourself.
Remember also those being mistreated, as if you felt their
pain in your own bodies. Give honor to marriage, and
remain faithful to one another in marriage. I'll surely judge
all people who are immoral and those who commit adultery.
Don't love money, be satisfied with what you have. I'll never
fail you or abandon you. I Am your Lord, your helper, have
no fear. What can mere people do to you? Remember your
leaders who taught you My Word. Think of all the good that
has come from their lives, and follow their example of faith.
I, Jesus, Am the same yesterday, today, and forever.

LORD, even though my mind can imagine all the 'what ifs,' only You know the true outcome of every circumstance, beginning to end. I'll let go of my vain imaginations and *put my trust in You.* You've proven it many times, when I was way off. So I'll rest and relax in the Light of Your loving Presence, knowing You are in control. I release all that concerns me to You, my Savior. I'll take hold of Your strong hand, because my hope and security are in You alone. I'm persuaded that *nothing can separate Us, and our great and eternal Love.* In Jesus' Name, Amen!

I Corinthians 10:10–13;
Hebrews 12:26–29

~

My child, do not grumble as some have done, and then were destroyed by the death angel. Things happened to them as an example to you. They're even written down to warn you who live at the end of the age. Just when you think you're standing strong, be careful not to fall. The temptations in your life are not any different than what others experience. And I Am faithful! I'll not allow the temptation to be more than you can stand. When you're tempted, I'll show you a way out so that you can endure. When I spoke from Mount Sinai, My Voice shook the earth, but now I make another promise: "Once again I'll shake not only the earth, but heaven also." All of creation will be shaken and removed, so that only unshakable things will remain. Since you'll be receiving an 'Unshakable Kingdom be thankful and please Me by Worshipping Me with Holy Fear and Awe! For I, your God, Am a Devouring Fire!'

LORD, my heart is forever grateful to You for all things, but mostly for my Jesus, giving His Life for my sins to be forgiven through His death, which gave me Salvation. My life is full and overflowing within as I realize what suffering He endured and My Savior and King "never gave up." I, too, will "never give up!" I see You, my Lord, in the awesome Light of Your Love, as my eternal purpose. I'll have a grateful attitude and walk in a place of gratitude toward the Life You've given me. I'll cultivate a grateful heart, and my days will be filled with one purpose, "to please You." Be glorified in me, my Lord, and fill me with Joyful Song; songs of deliverance, and songs of great hope that bring You Honor this very day. In Jesus' Name, Amen!

Lamentations 3:22–27; Isaiah 40:31; Psalm 16:11

꩜

My beloved, My faithful Love for you never ends! My mercies never cease! Great is my faithfulness; My mercies are fresh every morning. I Am your own inheritance; therefore, Hope in Me! I Am good to those who depend on, and who search for Me. It is good to wait in the quiet stillness, silence, for My Salvation. It is good to submit at an early age to My discipline. Trust in Me and you'll find 'New Strength.' You'll soar high on wings like eagles. You'll run and not grow weary, walk and not faint. Listen! I'll show you the way to live your life, granting you the Joy of My Presence and the pleasure of living with Me, forever!

LORD, I want to walk in the awareness of You continually, being aware of Your Voice and of Your lead. I trust You Lord, completely, Sometimes I blow it by just not seeing the opportunities You've placed right in front of me, until it seems to be too late. Teach me sharper discernment and a quick sense of my surroundings. I don't want to miss anyone that needs You. There are needs everywhere I go, and if they're ready, You know it. Stir up Your gifts in me for all the heart needs of those You place around me. I'll work on watching for others in my daily walk, no matter where I may be. It takes just a few moments of my time, but could mean the beginning of an eternal life for someone. *Lord,* here I am, *send me.* In Jesus' Name, Amen!

Philippians 2:12b–17

~

*My beloved, work hard to show the results of your salvation,
obey Me with deep reverence and fear. I Am working in you,
giving you the desire and power to do what pleases Me. Do
everything without complaining and arguing, so no one can
criticize you. Live clean innocent lives as My child. Shine
bright in a world full of crooked and perverse people. Hold
firm to 'My Word of Life, for on the day of Jesus' return,
you'll be proud that you did not run the race in vain,' and
that your work was not useless. Rejoice, even if you lose
your life, pour it out like a liquid offering to Me, just like
your faithful service is an offering to Me. I want all to share
in this Joy.*

LORD JESUS, my Savior, I thank you for pouring out your Life for me.
You've given Yourself, so that I can Live. I now want to give of myself to You
in abundance, even more today than yesterday. Staying aware, attentive to
You, ready to receive all that You'll pour into my innermost being, I'll run the
race that you've set before me. Lord, increase our intimacy, I want to know
You more. I'll Live my Life for You today, keeping watch for Your view, and
seeing others through Your 'Eyes of Love.' I will be in Your Perfect Peace
as I hold firmly to Your Word and watch for your return. My mind is on
You, and I Rejoice in knowing Your faithful Love, and lasting Joy! In Jesus'
Name, Amen!

Isaiah 26:2–4; Proverbs 23:15–16; Mark 10:14–15

᠗

My child, open the gates to all who are righteous; allow the faithful to enter. I will keep in perfect peace those who trust in Me, and those who keep their mind fixed on Me. Trust Me always for I, your Lord, Am your Eternal Rock! My child, if your heart is wise, My own heart will Rejoice! Everything in Me will celebrate when you speak what is right. Let all the children come to Me. Don't stop them! For My Kingdom belongs to those who are like these children. I tell you the truth, anyone who does not receive My Kingdom like a child, will never enter in.

FATHER, Your Word tells me that I am to *be anxious for nothing, but pray and be thankful.* I do, at times, stop myself from getting anxious by accepting my own limitations and taking it to You. Then, when I talk with You, giving You my full attention, You have this amazing way of bringing a clear more righteous view to all that concerns me. *'You bring heaven to earth'* and Peace like a river flows through me again. Lord, I, Your child, choose just to snuggle in close to You, feeling Your touch this morning as we share our thoughts, in intimate communication. Fill me up, Lord, fill my heart with more of You. That's all I ask for, that's all I really want. In Jesus' Name, Amen!

Proverbs 3:5; Jeremiah 29:11–13; Psalm 36:9–10; Proverbs 21:21

＞

My beloved child, trust Me with all your heart. Don't depend on your own understanding. Seek My Will in all you do, and I'll show you which path to take. I, your Savior, know the plans I have for you. They are plans for your own good and not for disaster, to give you a future and a hope. In those days when you pray, I'll listen! If you look for Me wholeheartedly, you'll find Me. I Am your Fountain of Life, the Light by which you see! I pour out My unfailing Love on those who Love Me, and I give justice to those with honest hearts. Pursue righteousness and you'll find unfailing Love, Life, Righteousness, and Honor.

FATHER, I do 'Trust You' in the depths of my heart, completely. You're my great delight, this day and always. I continually have situations in my life that prove Your faithfulness to me. Confirmations of Your direction for my life, and of Your Presence are all around me. If I'm looking for You, signs of Your intentions will be found and felt in every moment of my day. I ask You to open the heart of my eyes, so I might see more of You, my hidden, yet visible Treasure and Lord. "I put my Trust You, Jesus." In Your Ever-faithful Name, Amen!

Philippians 4:6–7, 13, 19;
II Corinthians 4:18

～

My beloved, don't worry about anything, instead talk to Me about everything. Tell Me about what you need, and thank Me for all I've done. Then you will experience My Peace, which exceeds anything you can understand. My Perfect Peace will guard your heart and mind as you live your life in Jesus, My Son. You can do everything because He gives you all the strength you'll ever need. This same One who takes care of you will supply all that you'll need from His glorious riches, which have been given to you by Jesus. So don't look at the troubles you see here on this earth now, but fix your view on things you cannot see 'yet!' For the things you see now will be gone, and the things you cannot see 'yet' will last forever!

LORD, Your promises are true, You meet all of my needs, faithfully. It may not always be in my timing, but Your timing is perfect! You bring to me Peace, and the patience I need to wait and trust You. And through all the waiting, when I come to You, I receive all I need to sustain me. In the quietness of the morning, You pour into me all, patience, hope, endurance, and preparation. You're my hiding place in the midst of it. Rid my heart, my Lord of all that does not please You. Shine Your Light within me so Your Peace will reign. I Thank You, Lord, for all times, good and even troubled times, because they're both for me to see my need for You. I'm changed within, growing closer, and stronger today. In Jesus' Name, Amen!

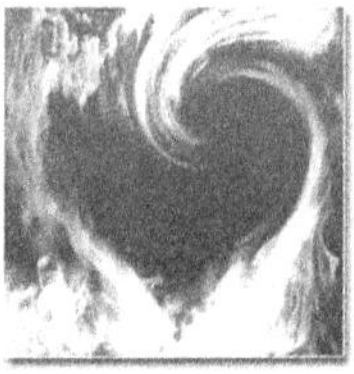

Ephesians 3:17–21

❧

My child, Jesus will make His home in your heart as you
trust in Him. Your roots will grow down deep in My Love
and keep you strong. You have the power to understand,
as My people should, how wide, how long, how high, and
how deep My Love is. You'll experience the Love of Jesus,
though it's too great to understand completely. You'll be
made complete, with all the fullness of life and power that
comes from Me. Give all Glory to Me, for I'm able, through
My Mighty Power at work in you, to accomplish infinitely
more than you ask or think. Give Glory to Me in the church
and in Jesus through all generations, forever!

FATHER, I know that *all things are possible to those who believe.* And that
with You, I can do all things. You have proven Your Strength and Your Love
to me again and again. So Lord, will You help my unbelief, and my concern
when it comes to those I love, making what seems to me to be, 'wrong choices.'
I realize that You've been at work on them and me, but some things seem like
they won't, *come together according to Your Word.* I put my hope and trust
in You alone. I'll draw in close, listening for Your voice and direction for me.
I'll watch You do the work that needs to be done. I'll keep my mind focused
on You, knowing that *all things work together for good to those who* love You,
and are called *according to Your purpose.* My life is in You Lord, no matter
what. Today and forever, I'm Yours! In Jesus' Name, Amen!

Psalm 116:17–19; Psalm 33:1–5; I John 1:7

❧

My beloved child, offer a sacrifice of thanksgiving and call on My Name. Fulfill your vows to Me in the presence of My people in My house, in the heart of Jerusalem. Praise Me! Let the godly sing with Joy to Me; it is fitting and pure to Praise Me. Praise Me with melodies on the lyre; make music for Me on a ten-stringed harp. Sing a new song of Praise to Me; play skillfully on a harp, and sing with Joy! For My Word holds true, and you can trust everything I do. I Love what is just and good; My unfailing Love fills the earth. If you live in the Light as I Am in the Light we'll fellowship with each other. My Son's blood cleanses you from sin.

LORD, I ask for Your forgiveness for the times when I've taken things, people, time, and even You for granted. I know that I have, even without realizing I did. I know now that staying in constant, intimate communion with You is the greatest way for me to avoid temptations Satan will try to entice me with. As I walk through the day, I'll worship You, my King, Praising You for all You are to me. I'll be reminded of the good things You've provided for me. I'll sing of Your goodness, keeping a song of praise on my lips, I'll practice thankfulness until it becomes a part of my DNA. I'll take the positive road of life even when all is not perfect, because in You, it is well with my soul. The Light of Your Presence is with me and I'm overjoyed, Hallelujah! In Jesus' Name, Amen!

Genesis 28:15; Hebrews 13:8–9, 15–16

～

My beloved, I Am with you, and I will protect you wherever you go. One day I'll bring you back to the land. I'll not leave you until I've finished giving you everything I've promised you. Remember the leaders who have taught you My Word. Think of all the good that has come from their lives, and follow the example of their faith. I, Jesus Christ, am the same yesterday, today, and forever. Don't be attracted by strange new ideas; your strength comes from My grace, not from rules about food, which won't help those who follow them. Therefore, offer through Jesus a continual sacrifice of praise to Me, your God, proclaiming allegiance to My Name. Don't forget to do good and to share with those in need. These are the sacrifices that please Me.

LORD, Your Companionship is my moment-by-moment desire. I chose to be near to You continually. When the day progresses and daily life happens, I find myself caught up in all the concerns of this world. Before I know it, I realize a lot of time has passed and I have not kept my eyes on You, but on my circumstances. I'm not sure exactly how to stop myself from doing this. But, I know I'll Press in and Press on until my whole identity is *'who I am in You.* I'll whisper Your Name, realizing I'm always prepared to receive from You.' I'll watch for You, staying in tune, and listening to hear the sound of Your voice. I'll not drift away, but cling to You, Jesus. I'll sing Praises to Your Name, declaring Your awesome goodness to all who come my way, from generation to generation, with a sacrificial and humble heart, always. In Jesus' Name, Amen!

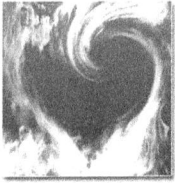

Romans 8:38–39; Exodus 33:14; Proverbs 8:33–35

❧

My beloved, be convinced that nothing can separate you from My Love. Neither death, or life, not angels or demons, not your fears for today, or your worries about tomorrow. Not the even the powers of hell can separate you from My Love. No power in the sky above or in the earth below; absolutely nothing in all creation will separate you from My Love that is revealed to you in Jesus Christ, My Son. I'll personally go with you; like Moses, I'll give you rest. Everything will be fine for you. Listen to My Wisdom and be wise. You'll be Joy-filled if you listen to Me, watching for Me daily at My Gates, waiting for Me. Whoever finds Me, finds Life and receives favor from Me.

FATHER, as I walk with You in the light of this day, remind me that You are there. Cause me to sense You more clearly, make my eyes to see, and my ears to hear. May Your Spiritual senses, be alive in me today. I ask for those giftings You've so graciously given, to be stirred up in me more today, that I may be all that I can be for You, my Savior. Let all the problems and concerns of this world become dulled to me when I am in Your Peace-filled Presence. I want to learn to know You more. My Life is an instrument of Your Love and Light. Your Peace is mine to Live in. *I choose to practice it today.* I ask You for favor and wisdom as I go! In Jesus' Name, Amen!

Psalm 118:24, 28–29;
Philippians 3:13–16

∾

My beloved, this is the day that I, your Lord, have made. Rejoice and be glad in it. I Am your God, Praise me! I Am your God, Exalt Me! Give thanks to Me for I Am Good! My faithful Love endures forever. No, My child, you haven't yet achieved it all, but focus on this one thing, forgetting the past and looking forward to what lies ahead. Press on to reach the end of the race and receive the heavenly prize for which I, through Christ Jesus, am calling you. Let all who are spiritually mature agree on these things. If you find you disagree on some point, believe that I'll make it plain to you. You must hold on to the progress you've already made.

LORD, I rejoice in Your loving Presence in my life this day. I'm blessed to have You in my life continually, and intimately. My heart and hands are open to receive from You, all that You chose to pour into me. I will not complain, for I know that Your desire is for my good, and not for evil. I put my trust in You my Savior, and my King. Any and all situations that come my way have already been okayed by You. I'll walk them out with You by my side, *'one day at a time, sweet Jesus!'* My time is in Your hands, for I've surrendered my time to You. My life is abundantly full in Your Presence today. You meet all of my needs according to Your Richness and Your Abundance of Glory and Grace day by day. In Jesus' Name, Amen!

Colossians 3:22–24; John 15:5; Psalm 105:3–4

∼

My child, obey your earthly masters in everything you do. Try to please them all the time, not just when they are watching. Serve them in all honesty, because of your reverent fear of Me. Work with honest integrity at whatever you do, as though you were working for Me, rather than for people. Remember that I, your Lord, will give you an inheritance as a reward; the Master you serve is Christ Jesus. I Am the Vine, you're the branch. If you remain in Me, I'll remain in you, and you'll produce much fruit. For apart from Me you can do nothing. Lift up My Name, rejoice as you Worship Me. Search for Me and for My strength, continually seek Me.

FATHER, as I sit in the quietness of the morning, aware of Your Presence all around me, I'm overjoyed. I feel completely victorious in You. As we share our heart-felt thoughts with each other, I give You my full attention, and I know I have Yours. As we intimately converse about everything, our lives merge into the Life of this day that You've provided. Whatever it holds, together with You, I can do all things. Fresh Joy and the Light of Your Love will consume the time You've set before me. As I walk with You close by my side, I know I am blessed, even in the day's tasks. I watch and listen for You, as You carefully ribbon Yourself intimately through the day, moment by moment. In Jesus' Name, Amen!

Hebrews 6:18–19

～

My beloved child, I have given both My Promise and My Oath. These two things are unchangeable, because it is impossible for Me to lie. Therefore, you who have fled to Me for refuge can have great confidence as you hold to the hope that lies before you. This hope is a strong and trustworthy anchor for your soul. It leads you through the curtain into My inner sanctuary. Jesus has gone in before you. He is your eternal High Priest, in the order of Melchizedek. There's an Oath regarding Jesus, My Son. For I've said to Him; I've taken an Oath and I'll not break My Vow: You're a Priest forever. Because of this Oath, Jesus is the One Who guarantees the better covenant with Me.

LORD, I grasp hold of Your strong hand as I sit here quietly with You. The comfort of Your Light and Love are to my heart, what I imagine our home in heaven will be. I find that as I speak with You about our Life's journey, the deepest corners of my heart are in communion with the whole concept of heaven in Your loving Presence. I'm in awe of all the possibilities that holds. I realize I see Your amazing heart in the things here on earth that You have created for Your Glory. They all cause my heart to praise Your matchless Name. I try to imagine 'Heaven' with You, and I say, "Prepare me Lord, make me ready for that wonderful day. Don't let me miss anything You have for me along the Life-path that You've given, so graciously to me. I Thank You! I Love You Lord!" In Jesus' Name, Amen!

Matthew 21:21–22; Psalm 31:14–16; Psalms 37:3–5, 7b

⁓

My beloved, Jesus says: "I tell you the truth, if you have faith and don't doubt, you can do things like I've done and much more. You can even say to this mountain, 'may you be lifted up and thrown into the sea,' and it will happen. You can pray for anything, and if you have faith, you will receive it." Trust in Me, I Am your God! Your future is in My hands. I rescue you from those who hunt you down relentlessly. My favor shines on you, My servant. And in My unfailing Love, I your God, rescue you. Trust in Me and do good. Then you will live in the land and prosper. Take delight in Me, and I'll give you your heart's desire. Commit everything you do to Me. Trust Me, and I will help you. Be still in My Presence, and wait for Me to act.

FATHER, teach me to trust You completely. I want to know how to continually keep trusting in You. No matter what my circumstances are, You are aware of all. You've already planned it all out. I'll find a place, where we can be alone, and *I'll quietly 'listen.'* You have intimate instructions for me today. You'll not only give me direction, but comfort and Joy. Then, You'll give me the grace and Peace I'll need for the journey. My Life has become an adventure with You. You set me up for assignments with others, on Your behalf. You make my life an exciting blessing with outrageous outcomes. Each new day is unlike any day before. Because I know You, I choose to put my trust in You. My desire is that You can trust me too, all the days *of my life.* In Jesus' Name, Amen!

Isaiah 12:2–6; II Corinthians 13:5

My beloved, see I've come to save you. Trust Me, don't be afraid. I, your God Am your Strength and your Song. I've given you Victory! With Joy you'll drink deep from the fountain of My Salvation! In that 'wonderful day' you'll sing: "Thank You Lord! Praise His Name!" Tell the nations what I've done, let them know how Mighty I Am! Sing Praise to Me, for I've done marvelous things. Make known My Praise around the world. Let all the people of Jerusalem shout My Praise with Joy! For Great Am I, the Holy One of Israel who lives among you. Examine yourself to be sure that your faith is genuine. Test yourself, surely you know that My Son Jesus is among you. If not, you'd fail the test of genuine faith.

FATHER, my complete confidence is in You alone. I know You're my Strength, my Shield, and my Strong and Mighty Tower. My faith and my Life are in You alone. When circumstances arise that are simple, or difficult, I've learned to take them all to You. With an intimate trusting heart, I ask for discernment to know just what to do. You've never failed to give me direction and show me what my part is. Of this I'm sure, Your ways Lord are higher than mine and my heart ready to say; 'Yes' to Your will. I'll follow You! I grasp Your hand with mine and You Lord, take the lead. You're Love and Light are causing me to 'be ready' for Your Kingdom. I'm pressing onward and upward in Your Presence today. In Jesus' Name, Amen!

II Corinthians 12:9–10; 8:8–9; Proverbs 23:15–16

❧

My beloved, My Grace is all you need. My Power works best in weakness. So you'll be glad to boast of your weaknesses, that My Power in Christ can work mightily through you. That's why you take pleasure in your weaknesses, and in insults, in the hardships, persecutions, and troubles that you suffer for Christ Jesus, My Son. When you're weak, I Am Strong! You can not oppose the truth, but you must always 'Stand for the Truth.' You're glad to seem weak if it helps show that you're actually strong. Pray that you'll become mature. My child, if your heart is wise, My Own Heart will rejoice! Everything in Me will celebrate when you speak what is Right!

LORD MY GOD, I desire to walk with You in a humble and a respectful way. Having a heart of thankfulness that is worthy of You, is my desire ever day. I'm not sure that I always show just how thankful I am, but my gratitude would take more than a life time, even an eternity to express. "You're my everything, Lord!" Your loving Presence is my greatest delight. Daily I'm more aware of You and less aware of my own desires and concerns. That's the way I believe I should be. You know my every need and You control the universe by Your Great Power. Make me an instrument of Your Peace. I'll walk through the day as a funnel, and a reflection of Your Love in this world that so desperately needs You, following Your lead, close by Your side, with a thankful heart today. In Jesus' Name, Amen!

Isaiah 41:10–13; Ephesians 1:10–11

~

My child do not be afraid, for I Am with you. Don't be discouraged, for I Am your God. I'll strengthen you and help you. I'll hold you up with My Victorious right hand. You see, all your enemies lie there, confused and humiliated. Anyone who opposes you, will die and come to nothing. You'll look in vain for those who tried to conquer you. Those who attack you will come to nothing. For I, your God, hold you by your right hand. I am the Lord your God. And I say to you: "Do not be afraid, I Am here to help you!" At just the right time, I'll bring everything under the authority of Jesus, My Son; everything in Heaven and on earth. Also, because you're united with Jesus, you've received an inheritance from Me. I've chosen you in advance, and I make everything work out according to My Plan.

LORD, in the quietness of the day, I'm aware of Your Presence. I'll stay aware of You, even as the sounds of life arrive and try to drown out the quiet of my time with You. You're still here drawing me by Your Spirit unto Yourself. If I watch and listen for You, I can be comforted by Your Peace continually. No matter what is going on around me, You'll show me where my portion is and where I can best serve You. I'll respond to whatever comes my way with a steady, confident, and loving attitude. Then I can be a reflection of Your Light. In You Lord, I live and move and have my being. I'll rejoice with Your goodness. *I Believe in You, and I will never give up!* In Jesus' Name, Amen!

Philippians 4:4–7, 13, 19; Hebrews 4:16; Psalm 105:1–3

❧

My beloved, don't worry about anything; instead, pray about everything. Tell Me what you need, and thank Me for all I've done. Then you'll experience My Peace, which exceeds anything you can understand. My Peace will guard your heart and mind as you live your life in Jesus Christ, My Son. You can do everything in Him, because I give you Strength. I, the same God who takes care of you, supplies all your needs from My Glorious riches, through Jesus. So, come to My Throne boldly. I Am your gracious God, in Me you will receive Mercy, and you'll find Grace to help when you need it most. Give thanks to Me and proclaim My Greatness! Let the whole world know what I've done. Sing to Me, Yes, Sing My Praises! Tell all about My wonderful deeds. Exalt My Holy Name, Rejoice, and Worship Me!

FATHER, Your Peace is here with Me this very moment, and I'm confident it will be with me through this day. As I keep my heart and mind in intimate communion with You, Your abundant Love is ever here for me. I can share this Great Love of Yours with others, because it only grows sweeter, and it never ends. I'm aware of my need for You whenever I have concerns in my day. I'm so confident that You'll make a way for me, even if there seems to be no way from my view. You have everything already worked out and Your outcome is always outrageous! Lord, Your Grace is more than sufficient for me, and Your sweet Mercy endures forever. I Thank You for all of Your promises, my Savior. I will exalt Your Holy Name Forever! In Jesus' Name, Amen!

Jeremiah 31:3; Psalm 32:6–10; Psalm 107:8

~

My beloved child, long ago I said to Israel; "I've Loved You My people, with an everlasting Love. With unfailing Love I've drawn you to Myself." Therefore, let all the godly pray to Me while there's still time, that they'll not drown in the floodwaters of judgment. I Am your hiding place, I protect you from trouble. I surround you with songs of Victory! I'll guide you along the best pathway for your life. I'll advise you, and watch over you. Don't be like a senseless horse, or a mule, that needs a bit and bridle to keep it under control. Many sorrows come to the wicked, but unfailing Love surrounds those who trust Me. Let all Praise Me for My Great Love and for the wonderful things I've done for them all!

FATHER, though I know Your Love for me is eternal, and Your Presence is here with me always, it is hard not to measure from an earthly perspective. The unfailing Love of You, my Savior is unlike earthly love, and beyond my human understanding. I'm learning the depths of it day by day, and the reality of Your Love is overwhelming. Only You can transform my perspective, causing my world view to become heavenly. What I do in serving You, does not change the amount of Love You have for me, but it deeply changes me. May all Blessings, and Honor, and Glory be Yours forever, in all the days of my life. In Jesus' Name, Amen!

Leviticus 10:3; Mark 4:30–32; Deuteronomy 31:6; Psalm 73:23–24

❧

My beloved child, I'll display My Holiness through you who come near Me. I'll display My glory before all people. How can I describe My Kingdom? What story should I use to illustrate it? It's like a mustard seed planted in the ground. It's the smallest of all seeds, but it becomes the largest of all garden plants; it grows long branches, and birds can make nests in its shade. I use many similar stories and illustrations to teach you as much as you can understand. "Be strong and courageous! Don't be afraid, and don't panic. I, your Lord, will personally go ahead of you. I'll not fail you or abandon you." You still belong to Me and I hold your right hand. I guide you with My counsel, leading you to My glorious destiny!

FATHER, Your assurance and Peace are my constant friends. Our intimate conversation is pure Joy. In the still moments, You visit my heart with Your mercy and grace. No matter what is going on, You are here for me always. Though the world shakes and shudders around me, I have *Your Peace, the Peace that passes all understanding.* When I've put my faith and hope in You, I'm courageous! It's my choice to believe, and to trust, knowing *You will never leave me or abandon me.* Though I don't know what the future holds, I know You do hold my future. My life is in Your hands, and You take care of my every need. I'll search Your Word to fill my heart and mind with more of Your wisdom and knowledge. Your steadfast Love for me is true. Your Strength and Joy fill my heart, as I Live my Life for You today. In Jesus' Name, Amen!

I Corinthians 1:10; Psalm 27:1; Romans 8:1, 2, 6; Proverbs 19:22–23

❧

My beloved child, appeal to Me by the authority of Jesus, My Son. Live in harmony with each other. Have no division in the church. Be of one mind, be united in thought and purpose. I, your Lord, Am your Light and your Salvation, so why be afraid? I'm your Fortress, protecting you from danger, so why tremble? Now remember this, there is no condemning those who belong to My Son. Because you belong to Him, the Power of My Life-giving Spirit has freed you from the power of sin that leads to death. Letting your sinful nature control your mind leads to death. But, letting My Spirit control your mind leads to Life and Peace. Loyalty makes a person attractive. It's better to be poor than dishonest. Your fear of Me leads to Life, bringing security and protection from harm.

LORD RENEW MY MIND TODAY, I surrender it to You, all of its thoughts and plans. I want Your will, not my own, to be my focus. Again Lord I say; renew my mind and make me an instrument of Your Peace, to be used by You for Your Glory, everyday. I'll join my heart with Yours, fearlessly, I'll be a risk-taker and a disciple-maker. Pleasing You is my one desire and hope. You died for me, my Jesus, so I will live only for You. Fulfill Your plans and purposes in and through me. I chose to open my mind and heart, allowing Your thoughts and ways to become mine. I was created in the likeness of Your image, to be filled with Your Light and Life. *I do surrender all, Lord, I am Ready! What is Your assignment for me this day? Let's go together and do it!* In Jesus' Name, Amen!

John 8:34–36; Proverbs 19:20–21; John 10:27–30

≈

*My beloved, I tell you the truth, everyone who sins is a slave
of sin. A slave is not a permanent member of the family,
but a son is part of the family forever. So if My Son sets you
free, you're truly free. Get all the advise you can, so you'll be
wise the rest of your life. You can make many plans, but My
purposes will prevail. My own sheep 'listen' to My Voice,
I know them, and they follow Me. I give them eternal Life,
and they'll never perish. No one can snatch them away
from Me, for I've given them to My Son, and I'm more
Powerful than anyone else. No one can snatch you from My
Hand. I, and My Son are One!*

LORD, the *'what if's'* are sometimes out of control in my mind, and the
minds of those around me. When I think about how so much of my time
has gone into nowhere thoughts and that all I have is a lack of peace, and *'no
real answers.'* It's in these instances I realize the depths of my need to stay
in intimate communication with You. Praying continually, keeps my mind
from getting caught up in a whirlwind of negative nothings. I've decided to
trust You completely my Savior. It is You whose brought me through every
circumstance in my life, safe and secure. I want to hear Your awesome Voice,
and just sit in the quietness at rest in You. This is where Your perfect Peace
abides, and abundant life is mine to obtain one moment at a time. I'll listen
and watch in Peaceful rest, for Your plans and Your purposes for me today.
In Jesus' Name, Amen!

Psalm 16:9–11; Romans 8:11, 15–16, 23

My beloved child, no wonder your heart is so glad, and you Rejoice. For your body is resting safely. I'll not leave your soul among the dead or allow My holy one to rot in the grave. I'll show you the way of life, granting you the Joy of My Presence, and the pleasures of living with Me forever. My Spirit, who raised Jesus, My Son, from the dead, Lives in you! And just as I raised My Son from the dead, I'll give Life to your mortal body by the same Spirit living within you. You've not received a spirit that makes you a fearful slave. But, you received My Spirit when I adopted you as My Own child. Now you call Me 'Abba Father.' My Spirit joins with your spirit to affirm that you're My child. You have My Holy Spirit in you as a foretaste of future Glory, and you long for your body to be released from sin and suffering. Wait with eager hope for the day when I'll give you your full rights as My adopted child, including the new body I promised you.

FATHER, this day that You have made is beginning so beautifully; in the silence I can hear the sound of You. I enjoy the stillness of our intimate time, and conversational exchange, where You equip and empower me for the day ahead. Each time I sit with You, I find that I'm able to 'stand' in authority and 'Love,' taking on the true image of Your Son, in every circumstance. You my Lord, are always there for me, ready to speak into my heart your answers to my many questions, or assignments I'm approached with. I avoid making wrong decisions and choices when I allow You to make them all for me. Your ways are wiser than mine, and in Your Presence I have fullness of Joy. My time is in Your Strong and Giving hands, and I have all I need in You. I'll do all You've called me to with excellence today! In Jesus' Name, Amen!

Psalm 46:1–2, 10;
II Corinthians 6:14, 17; Romans 8:1–2

My beloved, I Am your Refuge and Strength, ready to help when you're in trouble. You will not fear when earthquakes come and the mountains crumble into the sea. "Be still, and know that I'm your God! I'll be honored by every nation. I'll be honored throughout the world." Do not team up with those who are unbelievers. How can righteousness be a partner with wickedness? How can Light live with darkness? Therefore, come out from among unbelievers, separate yourself from them. For now there's no condemning you who belong to My Son, Jesus. Because you belong to Him, the Power of My Life-giving Spirit has freed you from the power of sin that leads to death.

FATHER, I fear not because I know that You are with me. You comfort me, and give me perfect Peace. I love the quietness I find with you, where I learn of Your Glory and Your Love. I'm at rest in the stillness of our intimacy, and our sweet conversations. Ours is a trust that transcends all time. It's being built up within me. I know I can trust that you're ever with me, and you'll never forsake me. Even in this earthly vessel, I'm becoming more trustworthy to You. This gives me overwhelming Joy, *the unspeakable and full-of-Glory kind of Joy!* To know that You trust me, makes all of my life worth living. I live because of You and *I live for You, my Savior and my King, today.* In Your Name, Jesus, Amen!

Hebrews 12:1–3, 12–13

❧

*My child, since you're surrounded by such a crowd of
witnesses to your life of faith, strip off every weight that
slows you down, especially the sin that so easily trips you up.
So now run with endurance the race I've set before you. Do
this by keeping your eyes set on Jesus, your Champion, who
initiates and perfects your faith. Because of the Joy awaiting
My Son, He endured the cross, disregarding the shame. Now,
He's seated in the place of Honor beside My Throne. Think
of all the hostility He endured from sinful people, then you
won't become weary and give up. So take a new grip with
your tired hands and strengthen your weak knees. Mark out
a straight path for your feet so those who are weak and lame
will not fall, but become strong.*

FATHER, at times the circumstances around me seem to be completely out
of my ability to control, or even attempt to fix. But You, Lord, are always in
control and not a thing that comes my way takes you by surprise. You knew
it all before the foundation of the world, amazing. You planned out all my
days, for my good, and for Your Glory, Your intention for my life. I want to
live in this place of knowing that even Jesus' Words were, *"Father, if you're
willing, please take this cup away from me. Yet, I want Your will to be done,
not mine."* This is my heart's desire, to look at every circumstance that comes
my way with complete trust and surrender, knowing that Your plan must be
fulfilled in and through my life today, *and it will!* In Jesus' Name, Amen!

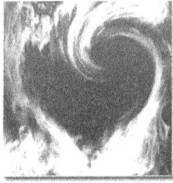

II Corinthians 4:16–18; Psalm 89:15

*My beloved child, this is why you should "never give up!"
Though your body is dying, your spirit is being renewed
every day. Your present troubles are small and won't
last very long. Yet, they'll produce in you a glory that
vastly outweighs them and will last forever! Don't look
at the troubles you can see now, instead, fix your gaze
on things that you cannot see. The things you see now
will soon be gone, but the things you cannot see will last
forever. Righteousness and justice are the foundations
of My Throne. Unfailing Love and truth walk before Me
as attendants. Happy are you who hear the joyful call to
worship, for you'll walk in the Light of My Presence.*

MY LORD, when I look to You, within my heart, I'm truly free. I'm free
to rest in the fact that I'm Yours, You're mine, and nothing will change that.
No need, no problem, and no tragedy, can separate the intimate communion
we now have. My response to these things can cause me *to feel* that You're
far away, or they can instantly draw me closer to Your Peace. The choice is
totally up to me. Where is my heart's identity? Is it in You? I've asked myself
these questions, because my responsibility is to know where my heart is. As
I turn toward You, the Light of Your Love and Your Presence are there to
shine on me and give me Peace. My Lord, You never change, but You're
continuously changing me into Your image. I'm thankful for the changes in
my life today. In Jesus' Name, Amen!

Psalm 121:1–3; II Samuel 22:14–17; Isaiah 40:31

❧

My beloved child, look up to the mountains, "Does your help come from there?" Your help comes from Me alone, I, who made heaven and earth. I'll not let you stumble; I, the One who watches over you, will not slumber. I, the Lord Most High, Thunder from heaven and My Voice Resounds. I shoot Arrows and scatter My enemies, My Lightning flashes and they're confused. Then at My command, at the Blast of My Breath, the bottom of the sea can be seen, and the foundations of the earth are laid bare. I reach down from heaven and rescue you and draw you out of deep waters. Those who put their trust in Me will find new strength, and soar high with wings like eagles.

LORD, I come to you in complete abandonment. My heart is ready for more of You, and my life-walk depends on You, for strength. I come to You today and You fill me up. Your grace and mercy surround me. My heart is overflowing with Love as I sit quietly with You in intimate communion. Lord, in these quiet moments I find rest. May Your Peaceful Presence be illuminated to me, and in me, as I walk with You through this day. I'm an instrument for You, my Savior. Use my life to express Your Light and Love to others, and I'll be blessed and changed from the abundance of it all. I'm Yours and You're mine. In Jesus' Name, Amen!

Lamentations 3:22–32

❧

My child, My faithful Love never ends! My mercies never cease. Great is My Faithfulness; My mercies begin fresh each morning. Remind yourself that I Am your Inheritance, Hope in Me! I Am good to those who depend on and search for Me. It's good to wait quietly for Salvation from Me. And it's good for people to submit at an early age to the yoke of My discipline. Sit alone in silence beneath My demands. Lie face down in the dust, for there will be hope at last. Turn the other cheek to those who strike you, and accept the insults of your enemies. No one is abandoned by Me forever. Though I bring grief, I also show compassion because of the Greatness of My unfailing Love.

FATHER, I trust You! I know at times I slip and find myself trying to make decisions about all that concerns me without first checking in with You. Then You always so sweetly urge my heart back unto Yourself. I am moved by You, I turn my focus back to the One who knows me best, and Loves me most. Your Peace comes in to flood my soul. Your loving Presence is where I find my rest from the storms of this daily life that try to drown me. You, Lord, calm the storms, reminding me that I am Yours, and You, Lord, are mine. I must learn to trust that You'll never leave me or let me down. You may allow difficulties in my life, but like the good things You bring my way, they're all for my own transformation and preparation for this day. In Jesus' Name, Amen!

Psalm 119:103–108;
I Peter 1:5a, 10–11

❧

My beloved, how sweet My Words taste to you, they're sweeter than honey. My commandments give you understanding; no wonder you hate every false way of life. My Word is a Lamp to guide your feet and a Light for your path. You've promised again and again to obey My righteous regulations. You've suffered much, but I, your Lord, will restore your life again, as I promised. I'll accept your offering of Praise, and teach you My regulations. Make every effort to respond to My promises. My beloved, work hard to show that you really are among those I've called and chosen. Do these things for Me and you'll never fall away. And I'll give you a grand entrance into My eternal Kingdom one day.

FATHER, the natural things of this world, I know are Your own creations. I'm finding they're perfect parables that explain to me, the truth of Your purposes. It's my responsibility to watch for You to explain them, then to understand them by Your revelation of their truth. I'll Listen, and understand more clearly as I 'See' You reveal them to me, with confirmation. Your awesome Presence in this amazing classroom called Life is my one true focus. And Your Word is my study book. As I eat of it's wisdom I grow in understanding of it's truth. Because of this, I need not be ashamed. Your Word is being written on the tablets of my heart and it's put there and reminds me, by Your Spirit, that I need it's truth, like a Light for the path of my Life. I do thank You, Lord, for Your Word! In Jesus' Name, Amen!

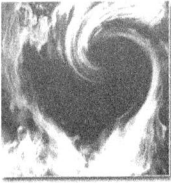

James 1:2–6; II Corinthians 12:9

My beloved child, when troubles come your way, consider it an opportunity for great joy. For you know that when your faith is tested, your endurance has a chance to grow. So let it grow, when your endurance is fully developed, you will be perfect and complete, needing nothing. If you need wisdom, ask Me, your generous Father and I'll give it to you. I'll not rebuke you for asking. When you ask Me, be sure that your faith is in Me alone. Do not waiver; a person with divided loyalty is as unsettled as a wave of the sea that's blown and tossed by the wind. My Grace is all you need. My Power works best in weakness. So now, be happy to boast about your weaknesses, so the Power of Jesus, My Son, can work through you.

FATHER, I know Your Word promises that in my weaknesses, You're my Strength. It also tells me that Your Joy, Lord, is also my Strength. As the time in my life-walk with You has gone by, I've come to learn the truth of Your promises. You're with me, in every moment of my day, to give me hope and fill my heart and mind with the wisdom of Your truth. My part is to read Your Word daily, and to listen for Your voice. I'll watch for You, spending my time in Your Presence. Then Your perfect Peace will be mine as I become more aware of You. I now know that the same Power that conquered the grave, Lives in me today! I can now walk with You in authority and Love. Wow, it's just as You exampled for me, my King. In Jesus' Name, Amen!

Luke 12:21–26, 31; Luke 1:78–79

◞

My child, a person is a fool to store up earthly wealth, but not have a rich relationship with Me. That's why I tell you not to worry about everyday life, whether you have enough food to eat or clothes to wear. Life is more than food, and your body more than clothing. Look at the birds, they don't plant, or harvest, or store food, yet I feed them. You're far more valuable to Me than birds. Can all your worries add a moment to your life? If worrying can't accomplish a little thing like that, what's the use of worrying about bigger things? Seek My Kingdom above all else, and I'll give you everything you need. Don't be afraid, little one, for it gives Me great happiness to give you the Kingdom! Because of My tender mercy, the morning light from heaven is about to break on you, to give light to those who sit in darkness and in the shadow of death, and to guide you to the path of Peace.

FATHER, when I think of all the time that has gone by, I'm in awe of the deepness of our intimacy Now. I'm ever so grateful to You for the 'who I am today,' because of the continued communion I've grown to walk in with You. Your Light and Love are in me, and with me, wherever I go, and our hearts are intimately connected. Today is what matters Now! Because, this is the day that You've made, I'll live in it, rejoice in it, and be glad for it, *Now!* I'll walk through this day watching You as You direct my steps. I'm carefree in You, my Jesus, because *You care for me.* I chose to keep walking today, in Your path of Peace for me. In Jesus' Name, Amen!

Proverbs 29:25; John 10:9–10; Isaiah 12:3–6

≈

My child, fearing people is a dangerous trap, but trusting Me means safety. Yes, I Am the Gate! Those who come in through Me will be saved. They'll come and go freely and will find good pastures. The thief's purpose is to kill, steal, and destroy. My purpose is to give you a rich and satisfying Life. With Joy you drink deeply from the fountain of salvation! In that day you'll sing, "Thank You Lord! Praise Your Name!" "Tell the nations what I've done. Let them know how Mighty I Am! Sing to Me, because I've done wonderful things. Make known My Praise around the world. Let all the people of Jerusalem Shout My Praise with Joy! Great Am I , the Holy One of Israel, who Lives among you."

LORD, I want to live my life fully dependent on You. Being close to You, is my hearts desire. Through easy days, and tough times, my prayer is that my mind would remain focused on the awareness of Your loving Presence. The knowledge that You're my Strength, and my Everything, is what keeps me going. As I've continued to remain aware of Your Presence around me, I know that I can do all things. Nothing can touch my life that is not first approved by You, my Savior. The kind of freedom this gives me is strength to my bones and peace to my soul. When I find myself lost and discouraged, I simply quiet my heart and listen, soon I hear Your gentle voice and I'm aware that You never left me. You'll never forsake me, never. As I draw closer to You, You fill me up with Your abundant Life and Joy that changes me, and flows to others. This is a blessing from You, flowing like a river within me. I only need to believe and receive from Your abundance, today. In Jesus' Name, Amen!

Intimacy Today: His Heart – My Heart

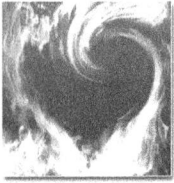

Matthew 6:24; Revelation 2:2–3; Ephesians 3:16; Psalm 16:11

❧

My beloved child, you cannot serve two masters. You'll hate one and love the other. You'll be devoted to one and despise the other. You cannot serve both Me and money! I know all the things you do. I've seen you work so hard, and your patient endurance. I know you won't tolerate evil people. You've examined the claims of those who say they're apostles but are not. You've heard their lies, and you've patiently suffered for Me without quitting. Now Pray, that from My glorious, unlimited resources, I'll empower you with inner strength through My Spirit. I'll show you the way of life, granting you the Joy of My Presence and the pleasures of living with Me forever.

FATHER, I know that in these days of our walk together here in this world, I'm finding that my intimacy and continual conversations with You are my ultimate goal. *You're my One First Love!* My first thought as I wake up in the morning, and my last thought as I lay down to sleep at night. My heart's desire is You, my Jesus, all day long. If I find my mind is wandering around on negative things, I get quiet, 'listen for the sound of You,' and then I'm redeemed. Your tender Love and encouragement give me Strength and Joy. Your awesome Presence is my constant pleasure. I want to be a reflection of Your Peace, Mercy, and Love every moment of my day. In Jesus' Name, Amen!

Psalm 29:1–10; I Peter 1:8

༄

My beloved, Honor Me, my child. Honor Me for My Glory and Strength. Honor Me for the Glory of My Name and the splendor of My Holiness. My Voice echoes above the sea. My Glory Thunders over the mighty sea. My Voice is Powerful, and Majestic, it splits the mighty cedars, and shatters the cedars of Lebanon. I make Lebanon's mountains skip, and Mt. Hermon leap. My own Voice strikes with bolts of Lightning, and makes the barren wilderness quake, it twists the mighty oaks and strips the forest bare. In My Temple, everyone shouts out "Glory!" for I Rule over the floodwaters, and I Reign as King Forever! I, your Lord give My people strength and bless them with Peace. You Love Me, though you've never seen Me. Though you don't see Me now, you trust Me, and you rejoice with a glorious, inexpressible Joy.

FATHER, I sit here this day in the stillness of the morning light. My heart is longing to sing You a Love song, then all at once I feel Your Spirit arise within me, with 'Humming.' I then realize I'm humming the same tune, and I'm consumed with amazing Love as I know that we are in sweet communion. Intimately we're engaged and the world around is quieted by Your divine Presence; giving and receiving unexplainable Love that only comes from knowing the One who gave all that He could give, for me. You're my Savior and my King, the Only way to the Father, and my Bridegroom, Jesus. In Your Name, Amen!

Psalm 95:1–7; I John 1:5, 7

Come, Sing to Me, your Lord! Shout joyfully to Me, the
Rock of your Salvation. Come to Me with thanksgiving,
Sing songs of Praise to Me. For I, your Lord, Am Great,
the Greatest King above all gods. I hold in My Hands the
depths of the earth and the mightiest mountains. The sea
belongs to Me, for I made it. My Hands formed the dry land,
too. Come, worship and bow down, kneel before Me, your
Lord and Maker, for I Am your God! You're the one I watch
over, you're under My care. Listen to My Voice today! I Am
the Light, there's no darkness in Me at all. If you're living
in the Light, as I Am in the Light, then we have fellowship
with each other, and the Blood of My Son, Jesus, cleanses
you from all sin.

LORD, to You alone I am truly thankful. In Your Presence is complete Joy.
You provide all that I need, and You're the reason I live. You're the Light of
My life, my very present Help in times of trouble. You're the Light in the
darkness, and my Security when I'm in need. You're Strong, Mighty, and
Ready for battle. You take up my defense. I need not be offended, or ever
desire revenge, for vengeance is Yours, and You're my Avenger. My heart's
desire is to be a reflection of You, and You are Good. I'm at rest now, knowing
that my identity is in You. I'm confident of Your Love for me, and I'll never
have need of anything that You'll not provide. You my Lord, are in control.
I've put my trust in You, and I'm blessed. In Jesus' Name, Amen!

II Corinthians 4:15–18;
II Corinthians 5:3, 5, 7

❧

My beloved child, all this is for your benefit. As My Grace reaches more and more people, there'll be great thanksgiving, and I'll receive more Glory. This is why you'll 'never give up!' Though your body is dying, your spirit is being renewed every day. Your troubles now are small and won't last very long. Yet they'll produce for you a glory that far outweighs them and will last forever! So, don't look at the troubles you see now, rather focus on the things you cannot see. The things you see now will be gone soon, but the things you cannot see will last forever. For you'll put on a heavenly body, you'll not be a spirit without a body. I, Myself, prepared you for this, and as a guarantee, I've given you My Holy Spirit. Whether you're here in this body, or away from it, your goal is to be to Please Me!

LORD, I'm blessed just to sit in the quietness of the morning with You. I know there's a list of things that I'll do today, but I ask You, my Lord, to remind me later, so that I can focus, my heart on You now. In these moments of intimate communion we have now, all else is just things to accomplish and they will have to wait. Lord, I need this time of intimate conversational relationship with You most of all, in order to live a life of Peace. In Your loving Presence, I find the only real and lasting Peace to be found, and I need Your perfect Peace today. My mind is fixed on You, my heart is open, and I'll receive more from You in these moments than all the world could try to provide me in my entire lifetime. I sit here and listen, waiting quietly, worshiping in whispers and humming songs of Praise to You. Hosanna! In Jesus' Name, Amen!

II Timothy 2:21–22, 25–26

~

*My beloved child, if you keep yourself pure, you'll be a
special utensil for honorable use. Your life will be clean, and
you'll be ready for Me, your Master, to use you for every
good work. Run from anything that stimulates youthful
lusts. Instead, pursue righteous living, faithfulness, love,
and peace. Enjoy the companionship of those who call on
Me, your Lord, with pure hearts. Gently instruct those who
oppose the truth. Perhaps I'll change those people's hearts,
and they'll learn of My truth. Then they'll come to their
senses and escape from the devil's trap. For they've been
held captive by him to do whatever he wants. But you must
remain faithful to the things you've been taught. You know
these things to be true, for you know you can trust those who
taught you.*

LORD, Your true Peace is mine because I've learned to lean on You completely, depending on You, and putting my trust in You alone, Lord. You,
my Lord, have never failed to teach me what You know is for my own good.
Your outcome is always best, and I choose to wait patiently for it. I'll walk
through life with my hand in Your Hand, and my heart filled with Your
Light and Love, as an example to others of You. I'll trust You with a restful,
and fearless heart. I'll remain anxious for nothing, but in everything give
thanks to You, for You're my Provider, my Best Friend, and my Redeemer
forever! "I'm fearless and filled with Peace, because of You, everyday!" In
Jesus' Name, Amen!

Malachi 3:1–2b; Revelation 22:12; Psalms 150:1–6

My beloved, Look I Am sending you My Messenger and He'll prepare the way before Me. Then I, the One you're seeking will suddenly Come to My Temple! The Messenger of the covenant, whom you look so eagerly for, is surely Coming, the Lord of Heaven's Armies. Who will be able to endure it? Who will be able to 'Stand' and face Him when He appears? "Look, I Am Coming soon, bringing My Reward with Me to repay all people according to their deeds." Praise Me, in My sanctuary, and in My Mighty Heaven! Praise Me, for My Mighty Works, and unequaled greatness! Praise Me, with blasts of rams horns, with lyre and harp, the tambourine and dancing, strings and flutes, with the clash of cymbals, with loud and clanging cymbals. Let everything that has breath Praise Me, your Lord! Praise your Lord!

FATHER, I'm excited in the deepest parts of my spirit for the awesome days ahead, and yet I know there is much to Come. Abundance in so many ways will be mine as I come to You in our quiet intimate place of rest. I want to hear Your heartfelt dreams and desires my Savior. I want to know You more. I watch for You to move and I follow. I'll draw closer to Your side and cuddle there, resting in the warmth of Your Love engulfing me. What more could I need? Nothing has a greater value than this, nothing. Praise rises up inside my heart and I sing out my Life before You. May I be a sweet Sound of favor to You. May my spirit's passion for You make a loving Sound of my true feelings of gratefulness and of outrageous adoration! I'll Love You and serve You forever, My King! In Jesus' Name, Amen!

Galatians 6:4–10

*My beloved child, pay careful attention to your own work,
for then you'll get the satisfaction of a job well done, and
you won't need to compare yourself to anyone else. You're
responsible only for your own conduct. You've been taught
My Word, so you should provide for your teachers, sharing
all the good things with them. Don't be mislead, you cannot
mock My justice. You'll always harvest what you plant. If
you live only to satisfy your own sinful nature, you'll harvest
decay and death from that sinful nature. If you live to please
the Spirit, you'll harvest everlasting life from the Spirit. So
don't get tired of doing what is good. At just the right time
you will reap a harvest of blessings if you don't give up.
Whenever you have the opportunity, do good to everyone,
especially those in the family of faith.*

FATHER, this is the day that You've made, I choose to rejoice and be glad
in it. I'll trust You for the day, moment by moment. Step by step, all this day
holds for my life You've planned for my good and not for evil. I'll walk with
You through this day aware of this fact. I'm watching for Your fingerprints
and arms around me. Lord, I know that what you supply in this day is all
that is needed for the transformation of my heart. I say, "Yes! Yes Lord, Yes
to Your Will and Your Ways! I'll keep on watching for any opportunities,
assignments prepared by You for Your Glory from the beginning. I'll keep
remembering You and I'll never give up for the sake of the Cross of my Lord
and Savior, Jesus Christ. All Praise from my lips will be Yours forever and
ever, Hallelujah! In Jesus' Name, Amen!"

II Corinthians 5:7; Galatians 6:14–18

～

*My beloved, you should live by believing and not by seeing.
As for you, never boast about anything except the Cross of
your Lord, Jesus Christ. Because of the Cross, your interest
in this world has been crucified, and the world's interest
in you has also died. It doesn't matter whether you've
been crucified or not. What counts is whether you've been
transformed into My new creation. My Peace and Mercy
will be upon all who Live by this principle; for you are My
new people! From now on, don't let anyone trouble you
with all these things. For you bear on your body the scars
that show you belong to Jesus Christ My Son. Now His
Grace is with you!*

FATHER, walking by faith and not by sight is the most peaceful way to live this life. Faith in You and Your Spirit's Power in my life is both exciting and fulfilling. You've shown me Your desire to empower me, and to challenge my days with assignments from You, that cause me to walk close by Your side in Our continual intimate communion. This is where You want me to live. I know You want me to accomplish Your purpose and destiny in my life and the lives of those that You cause me to affect along the way. Thank You, Lord, for making my life an instrument of Your true Peace. It is a life made limitless, because of Your Holy Spirit, teaching and comforting me through Your Gifts, which You've fashioned in me by the power of Your Son, in Whose Name I proclaim, Amen!

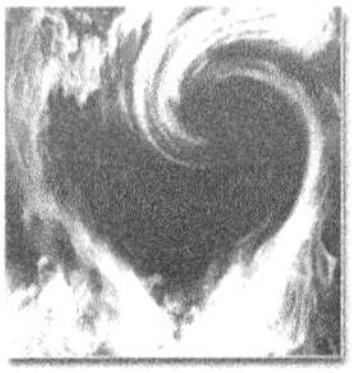

Psalm 103:11–19

My child, My unfailing Love is toward those who fear Me. It is great as the heights of the heavens above the earth. I'll remove your sins as far as the east is from the west. I Am like an earthly father should be to his own children, tender and compassionate to those who fear him. I know how weak you are, I do remember you are only dust. Your days on earth are like grass, like wildflowers, you bloom and die. The wind blows and you are gone as though you were never here. But My Love remains forever with those who fear Me. My Salvation extends to the children's children of those who are faithful to My Covenant and those who obey My Commandments. I, your Father, have made the heavens My Throne. From here I Rule over everything!

MY FATHER, I know your unfailing Love, Grace, and Your Mercy. You've provided me, everything I'll need to keep my Covenant with You, and to be obedient to Your Commandments. When I am weak, You, my God, are Strong in me and for me. I put my trust in You! When the winds blow and time flies by, I'll not be afraid, but I'll 'Stand' knowing that You are in Control and on Your Throne. I do not fear death for You are there! Nothing can touch me that You have not prearranged for my own good. You have in Your heart my seed and my seed's seed. No matter what, I'll remain faithful to You. For I know You intimately, You are the 'Lord of Heaven's Armies, My Savior, My Heavenly Father, and My King!' All that I need is in You! With my whole heart, I'll cling to You, because I Love You, intimately! In Jesus' Name, Amen!

II Samuel 22:29–37

My beloved, I Am your Lord and your Lamp. I Light up your darkness. In My Strength you can crush an army, and with Me you can scale a wall. My Way is Perfect! All of My Promises prove true. I Am a Shield for all who look to Me for protection. For who Am I except your Lord? Who but I Am a Solid Rock? I, your God, Am your Strong Fortress, and I make your way perfect. I make you as sure-footed as a deer. I enable you to 'Stand' on mountain heights.' I do train your hands for battle, and strengthen your arms to draw a bronze bow. I've given you My Shield of Victory! My help has made you great! I've made a wide path for your feet to keep you from slipping.

LORD, You are my Strength and my Shield! I can do all things with You. As I sit here in this quiet place, though there may be battles all around me, You're my Peace. In any storm of life, You're always there. Your Presence is where I find my sure footing. My foot rests on You, my Solid Rock of Grace. I Love You more than life itself. I long to linger at Your feet, and Listen to Your soothing Voice of confidence. I'll continue to 'Listen' and Watch for You. In our intimate communion, we'll accomplish, together, everything Your heart desires for this time and this day. I'll never fall, and never give up on You. In trust of Your plan, and in my Savior, Jesus' Name, Amen!

Proverbs 2:1–11

My beloved child, 'Listen' to Me and treasure My commands. Tune your ears to wisdom, and concentrate on understanding. Search for them as you would for silver. Seek them like hidden treasures. Then you'll understand what it means to fear Me, and you'll gain knowledge of Me. I, your Lord, grant you wisdom! From My Mouth come knowledge and understanding. I grant a treasure of common sense to the honest. I Am a Shield to those who walk in integrity. I guard the path of the just, and I protect those who are faithful to Me. Then you'll understand what is right, just, and fair, and you will find the right way to go. For wisdom will enter your heart, and knowledge will fill you with Joy! Wise choices will watch over you, and understanding will keep you safe.

MY FATHER, I will 'Listen' to You, for You are the One who holds wisdom in Your heart. You fill me with understanding as I come to You with a surrendered spirit, desiring more. In You is hidden Treasure designed just for Me. The knowledge You pour into me in our intimate time, is wisdom wrapped in Love, and it's Revelation to my soul. I'll speak out of the wisdom that You've already given, and I'll walk in the knowledge of Your pure truth. You, Lord, are a Shield encompassing about me. I'll strive for a heart filled with integrity as You give into me Your Grace. I'll be faithful to You, full of honesty, coupled together with wise choices. Your Mercy covers me as I 'Stand' ready to run with Joy and understanding, the awesome race You set before me today. You're my Strength, and my Great Reward, forever! Hallelujah! We Win! In Jesus' Name, Amen!

Matthew 5:43–48; Psalms 5:10–12

My beloved child, I know you've heard it said: 'love your neighbors and hate your enemies! But I say to you: "Love your enemies!" Pray for them that persecute you! This way, you'll be acting as true children of Mine. For I give My sunlight to both the evil and the good, and I send rain on both the just and the unjust. If you only Love those who love you, what reward is there in that? Even sinful people do that much. If you're only kind to your friends, what makes you different from anyone else? Even sinners do that. You're to be perfect, yes, even as I, your Father in heaven Am perfect. I'll declare guilt, not you! Let them be caught in their own traps. Then I'll drive them away because of their sins, for they've rebelled against Me, not you. I'll let all who take refuge in Me rejoice, and sing Joyful Praises forever! I'll spread My protection over them. All who Love My Name will be filled with Joy! I bless the godly and I surround them with My Shield of Love!

OH LORD, help me to Love the unlovely. Even those who bring hurtfulness upon those I love. I want to know how to Love as You Love in every circumstance. I realize that not always are those who hurt others acting in their own behalf, but at most times are driven by emotions and even by evil. You alone are their help. I'll pray to You on behalf of them. You're needed desperately, so that there will be a release, that they'll have freedom. Your salvation, revelation, and then surrendered hearts are the actions that will bring about freedom for all. Lord, by Your Holy Spirit, I pray that You'll draw them unto Yourself that they may be free to Love You first, and then find, in You, true and unconditional Love. I'm so grateful that You are my Savior and King, my Glory and the Lifter of my head. I know that You're protecting me, that You surround me like a shield. Nothing can touch me that You do not allow. I am Yours, and You're my Defender, now and forever. In Jesus' Name, Amen!

Isaiah 61:1–3; Philippians 2:3–5

～

My beloved child, I'm your Sovereign Lord and My Spirit is upon you. I've anointed you to bring good news to the poor. I've sent you to comfort the brokenhearted, and to proclaim that captives be released, that prisoners be freed, and the blind see. I've sent you to tell those who mourn, that the time of My Favor has come, and with it, the day of My Anger against their enemies. To all who mourn in Israel, I'll give a crown of beauty for ashes, a joyous blessing instead of mourning, festive praise instead of despair. In their righteousness, they'll be like great oaks that I've planted for My Own Glory! My child, don't be selfish, don't try to impress others. Be humble, thinking of others as better than yourself. Don't look out only for your own interests, but take interest in others, too. You must have the same attitude as My Son, Jesus.

FATHER, I say Yes, for I want Your Spirit to be upon me, living in me and through me. I'll go, and do, all that You desire of me without hesitation. You're my Sovereign King! I'll 'Go to the places You send me with my heart full of Your Glory and Grace. I'll tell of Your infinite Mercy, and I'll do whatever You ask me to! In humility, I'll go and share, not expecting anything in return, because You're my Reward. You Lord, give me all that I need in the coming and going. The needs of others must be met in order for Your Love expression to be evident to them. Let me be Your Love and Your Light to all that have need of You today and every day. May I have the attitude of My Redeemer, Jesus, in whose Name I Go, and I Pray, Amen!

Isaiah 61:8–10; Philippians 2:12b–13; Psalm 72:1

⌒

My beloved, I Am your Lord, and I Love Justice. I hate robbery and all wrongdoing. I'll faithfully reward My children for their suffering, and make an everlasting covenant with them. Their descendants will be recognized and honored among the nations. Everyone will realize that you're the children that I've blessed. You're overwhelmed with Joy, for I've dressed you in clothes of salvation and draped you in a robe of righteousness. You're like a bridegroom in his wedding suit or a bride with her jewels. Work hard to show the results of your salvation, always obeying Me with deep reverence and fear. For I'm working in you, giving you the desire and power to do what pleases Me. Give your Love of justice to Me, and righteousness to My Son.

LORD, as I have grown to know You and Your Justice, I, too, love it! You've taught me right from wrong in Your ways. Even in my own right and wrong choices, I've learned. You use them all to teach me, and You never leave me alone. Our everlasting covenant, and intimate relationship, keep me in close and deep communion with You. I'm overwhelmed with Joy. I'm understanding You more as my King. You surround me with Your Peace, and You drape me with Your Love, and righteousness. I'll stick close to You, obey You, and learn how to esteem You higher with deep reverence and fear, because You are Worthy! Work in me, all that is needed, and cause me to know, to do what pleases You. I Love Your Justice, and I'm more than grateful for Your Son, my Jesus, in Whose Name I say, Amen!

Deuteronomy 28:1–6, 13; Luke 11:28

My child, if you fully obey Me and carefully keep the commands I'm giving you today. I, your Lord, will set you high above all nations of this world. You'll experience many blessings if you obey Me. Your towns and fields will be blessed. Your children, your crops, and the offspring of your herds and flocks, your fruit baskets and breadboards, will be blessed. Wherever you go, and whatever you do, I'll bless. Yes, if you 'Listen' to the commands that I Am giving you today, and be very careful to obey them, I'll make you the head and not the tail. You'll always be on the top and never at the bottom. Even more blessed you'll be when you hear My Words and put them into practice!

MY FATHER, I'll be obedient to You at all times. I'll obey You, and follow Your commands for the day. I know that all I have need of, You provide. And You cause my labor to not be in vain. In Our time of quiet intimacy now, I'll 'Listen,' for You have deep desires for my life-path. Then as I'm in the moments of the day ahead, I'll watch for Your intentional intervention. As You show me the way, I'll follow hard after You. I'll remember Your Word, Your directions, and I'll put them into practice. For this is my longing, to fulfill Your will for me with Wisdom and with Grace, to bring You Joyful blessings as I fulfill my assignments with my mind and heart focused on You today. In Jesus' Name, Amen!

II Corinthians 3:2–6

∽

*My beloved, the only letter of recommendation you need
is yourself. Your Life is My letter written on your heart.
Everyone can read it and they'll recognize My own good
work in you. Clearly, you're a letter from Christ showing
the result of His Ministry in you. This 'letter' is not written
with pen or ink, but with My Spirit, I, your Living God!
It's not carved on tablets of stone, but on your human heart,
(your Character goes before you). You're confident of this
all because of your great trust in Me through Christ. And
it's not that you think of yourself as qualified to do anything
on your own. Your qualification comes through Me. I've
enabled you to minister of My New Covenant! Not of
written laws, but of the Holy Spirit. The old covenant ends
in death, but under the New covenant, the 'Spirit gives Life!'*

FATHER GOD, I thank You for Your Spirit that dwells in me Richly.
I know that without you, I'm like filthy rags. But with You, All things are
made New! My heart and mind are being transformed even now as I sit
here in a quiet place pondering all You are to me, and drinking in deep
what Your Word says I am in Christ Jesus, Your Son, and my Redeemer. I
want to be for You My God, a Light and a polished example of Your Love
toward others. You qualify me by Your transforming power in our intimate
times, as I chose to surrender my heart to You. This is when Your Words of
Life are written on the transparent tablets of my heart, and I become more
like a radiant representative of You. You cause this to change me into a New
creation, all the old passes away and I become New, in You. Lord, continue
this work in me that You will be glorified even more in my Life today! In
Jesus' Name, Amen!

Job 32:8–9; II Corinthians 3:16–18; Proverbs 22:8–9

❧

My beloved, My Spirit Lives within you. I, your Almighty God, give you breath within, this makes you wise. Sometimes the elders are not so wise. Sometimes the aged don't understand justice. But, whenever someone turns to Me, the veil is taken away. I, the Lord, Am the Spirit, and wherever I, and My Spirit are, there is Freedom! So all who have had that veil removed can 'See and Reflect My Glory.' I, your Lord, and My Holy Spirit, make you more like My Son, as you're being changed into 'His Glorious image.' Remember this; those who plant injustice, will harvest disaster, their evil will come to an end. But, blessed are those who are generous in justice, for they feed the poor.

FATHER GOD, I am so thankful for the comfort and guidance of Your Holy Spirit, who is my Teacher. You breathe Your breath of Life into me, and Your Spirit gives me wisdom to do all that pleases You. I can then walk in justice, understanding Your truth more moment by moment as Your plans for my daily life-path unfold before me. As we share together intimate conversations throughout the day, Your Spirit and Freedom will cause me to be a reflection of You. Your Greatness will touch others through me with a Love that will remove the veil that keeps them from Seeing Your Glorious image. Evil, and injustice will have to flee, and Your Freedom will feed the poor in Abundance today. Hallelujah! In Jesus' Name, Amen!

I Timothy 1:18–19; Jeremiah 29:11–12; I Timothy 2:5–6

≈

*My beloved child, the prophetic words spoken about you
earlier, may they help you fight well in My battle. Cling
to your faith in Jesus, My Son, and keep your conscience
clear. For some people have deliberately chosen to violate
their conscience, and as a result, their faith in Me has been
shipwrecked. Remember, My child, I say, "I know the
plans I have for you, My plans are for your good and not
for disaster. I give you hope, and a future." For you know
that there's only One God, that is Me, your Father, and One
Mediator who can reconcile Me with humanity, that is Jesus,
My Son. He gave His Life to purchase Freedom for everyone.
This message is given to the world at just the right time, and
My timing is perfect!*

FATHER, as I sit back and remember the prophetic words that have been
spoken over my life, I'm in awe of the big plans You have for me. At times
when You speak to me, things You have in Your heart for me, I'm amazed
at the way You trust me, yet my confirmed heart causes my faith in You
to soar to miraculous heights. One thing I want to be is secure of is that
I'll intentionally make choices in every situation that will not disrupt or
violate, in any way, my intimate communion with You. You're the One who
has given me Life. You've purchased my Freedom, and I chose to remain
Free! Your plans for my Life are my destiny, I'll not ever lose sight of them.
I'm 'watching and listening' closely for Your 'Sound and Light' to keep my
focused heart on You, always! In Jesus' Name, Amen!

I John 2:5–6, 15–17;
Proverbs 28:25–26

My child, if you obey My Word, you truly show how you Love Me completely. That's how you know you're living in Me. If you say you live in Me, you should live your life as Jesus did. Don't love this world or the things it offers you, because when you love the world, My love isn't in you. For this world offers only a craving for physical pleasure, a craving for all the things you see, and pride in your achievements and possessions. These are not from Me, but from the world. And this world is fading away along with all that people crave. But, if you do what pleases Me, you'll Live forever. Greed causes fighting, but trusting Me leads to prosperity. If you trust your own insight you're foolish, but if you walk in wisdom you're safe.

MY FATHER, I'll obey Your Word, and truly prove my Love for You. I want to walk in Your ways and Live in You. At times I may stumble and sway for an instant, but Your Holy Spirit is my guide, and will draw me back to my rightful place in You. My consistency with You is My greatest witness to those I love, and to those who are watching my life in the world around me. I'll resist the cravings of the world and follow after the Goodness of my God! Help me, my Lord, to resist the need for recognition and to simply trust You for Your reward. My hope is in You, my Savior, and You alone shall receive all the Glory, Honor, and Praise! You Alone are Worthy! I want to do only what pleases You. I'll follow after Your example for me, in my Jesus, trusting Your Holy Spirit's lead, and walking in the wisdom and truth you've given. I Surrender again! In Jesus' Name, Amen!

Proverbs 3:21–27; Psalm 16:5–6

～

My beloved child, don't lose sight of common sense and discernment. Hang on to them, for they'll refresh your soul. They're like jewels on a necklace. They keep you safe on your way, and your feet will not stumble. You can go to bed without fear, you'll lie down and sleep soundly. You need not be afraid of sudden disasters or the destruction that comes upon the wicked, for I, your Lord, Am your security. I'll keep your foot from being caught in a trap. Don't withhold good from those who deserve it when it's in your power to help them. If you can, help your neighbor now! I Am your Inheritance, I'm your Cup of Blessing. I guard all that is yours. The land I've given you is a pleasant land. What a wonderful inheritance!

MY FATHER, I'm in awe of You. You've gone before me on this path of life preparing the way of my inheritance in You. I'll not be afraid of anything that comes my way, but I'll trust You, because You've designed it all for my good. You're my Security, and my Vengeance, and nothing can keep me from Your protective Presence, nothing! You'll not allow me to fall as long as I put my trust and my hope in You. I'm thankful for my home, family, my friends, and neighbors, too. Cause me to be a blessing, Lord, for You, to everyone. Prompt me by Your Spirit whenever there's a need, but Lord, stop me when at times I may be a hindrance, instead. I'll keep my heart in this place of intimate talks with You. I'll be ready to hear Your instructions at just the right time. Oh, what blessings are in You for everyone. You, Lord, are our Inheritance. You're Savior, and King to all who believe and chose You, Now! In Jesus' Name, Amen!

Isaiah 50:4–5; Ephesians 4:30; Isaiah 54:17

~

My beloved, I, your Sovereign Lord, have given you My Words of wisdom, so that you know how to comfort the weary. Morning by morning, I wake you and open your understanding to My Will. I, your Sovereign Lord, have spoken to you, and you've 'Listened!' You've not rebelled, or turned away. Do not bring sorrow to My Holy Spirit by the way you live. Remember, I've identified you as my Own, guaranteeing that you'll be saved on the day of redemption. But in that coming day, no weapon turned against you will succeed. I'll silence every voice that rises up to accuse you. This benefit is enjoyed by My servants. Your vindication will come from Me. I, your Lord, have spoken.

MY SOVEREIGN LORD, and my Savior, You fulfill my every need. You cause me to rise up, and You also give me rest. When I awake in the morning, You, Lord, are there, patiently waiting and beckoning me. When I lie down to rest, You are there to comfort me and give me Peace, if I pay attention to You. When You speak to me, I'll 'Listen,' for You have much revelation to pour into my heart. I'll commune with You in quiet intimacy as I wake up, but even throughout the day, I'll listen for all opportunities to hear Your Voice of direction toward the greater things You have for me to do. I know that when I walk in Your Will and Purpose, nothing can stop me, nothing. My Lord, You are my Defender and my Peace. In Jesus' Name, Amen!

Proverbs 2:6–12;
Matthew 7:15, 16, 20; Psalms 9:7–8

Beloved, I, your Lord, grant Wisdom! From My Mouth come knowledge and understanding. I grant a treasure of common sense to the honest. I Am a Shield to those who walk with integrity. I guard the path of the just, and protect those who are faithful to Me. For you'll understand what is right, just, and fair, and you'll find the right way to go. For Wisdom will enter your heart, and knowledge will fill you with Joy. Wise choices will watch over you. Understanding will keep you safe. Wisdom will save you from evil people, from those whose words are twisted. So beware of false prophets who come disguised as harmless sheep, but are really vicious wolves. You can identify them by their fruit, that is, by their actions. Yes, just as you can identify a tree by it's fruit, so you can identify people by their actions. But I, your Lord, Reign Forever! I execute judgment from My Throne. I'll judge the world with Justice and Rule the nations with Fairness.

MY LORD, I come to You in intimate conversational communion. For I know where true Wisdom is found. You fill me with Your Truth, and Your Wisdom, which comes forth in my actions, and surprises me. Revelation flows from my lips, because of my surrendered time in Your awesome Presence. I cling to You, my Savior, and find myself being transformed by You there. I want to understand what Your heart's choices are for me. In order to understand more intentionally, I'll go to Your Word for the abundance of Wisdom I'll find within its pages. They Light my world and rock it! Let my actions continually reflect the fruit of time spent with You in our secret place of intimacy. You alone are my King! I'll Love You Forever! I'm completely Yours! In Jesus' Name, Amen!

Proverbs 4:10–13; Romans 6:19–21; Proverbs 19:20–21

≈

My child, 'Listen to Me,' do as I say, and you'll have a long, good life. I'll teach you wisdom's ways and lead you in straight paths. When you walk, you won't be held back. When you run, you won't stumble. Take hold of My instructions, don't let them go. Guard them, for they are the key to Life. Because of the weakness of your human nature, I use the illustration of slavery to help you understand it all. Before, you let yourself be a slave to impurity and lawlessness, which led even deeper into sin. Now you must surrender yourself to be a slave to righteous living, so you'll become Holy. You were a slave to sin, free from the obligation to do right. The result? You're now ashamed of the things you used to do, things that end in eternal doom. My child, get all the advice and instruction you can, so you'll be wise for the rest of your Life. You can make many plans, but My purposes for you will prevail.

MY LORD, I'll 'Listen intently' to Your wise advice and directions. I'll intentionally do, and speak, as You desire me too. You keep my path straight and make me strong and steady. I need Your Light and Love to carry me through all the way to the end. I've surrendered my heart and life completely to You. Our intimate conversations in the quiet, and in the midst of the noise, keep me aware of Your Presence surrounding me. I'm forgiven, and I'll walk in the place of freedom and right standing before You my Savior. Because of Your great Love for me, I'm unashamed of, and dead to my old ways, and to sin. I'm made right by You with my heart's surrender, and You have many purposes and plans that can now be fulfilled in me. Hallelujah! I'm Yours! In Jesus' Name, Amen!

Psalm 19:1–4, 7–11, 14

❦

My beloved, the heavens proclaim My Glory! The skies display My Craftsmanship. Day after day they continually speak, night after night they make Me known. They speak, not a sound or a word. Their voice is never heard. Yet their message goes throughout the earth, and their words to all the world. My Love, My instructions are perfect, reviving your soul. My decrees are trustworthy, making wise the simple. My commandments are right, bringing Joy to the heart. My commands are clear, giving insight for living. Your reverence for Me is pure, lasting forever. My laws are true, each one fair. More desirable than even the finest gold, sweeter than honey dripping off the comb. They're warnings to My servant, a great reward for those who obey. May the words of your mouth, and the meditation within your heart be a pleasing sound to Me, your Lord, your Rock, and your Redeemer!

OH MY LORD, there are so many things in this world that prove Your awesome truths. Your Love for me is so evident in the beauty that I see, and the vastness that You've provided. I'm filled with Worship within when I take time to ponder all that has been provided to show off to the world who You are. Father, You've provided all that we need to find our way to You. Jesus, You are for us, a Perfect Picture of a Surrendered Life. I want to be like You. I'll walk this life-path in as perfect communion with You as I can. I'll draw closer to You daily, dying to myself, picking up what's on Your heart for today and pressing on to do Your perfect will. Your pleasure in me is my reward, and I meditate on You daily. I feel deep within my own heart, the quiet Sounds of You, my Savior, and my King! Your Words fill my soul with Your Goodness, and Your Light and Love are embracing me, today. In Jesus' Name, Amen!

Proverbs 4:20–23;
II Corinthians 9:7–9, 11–12

❧

My child, pay close attention to what I say. "Listen carefully to My Words." Don't lose sight of them, but let them penetrate the deepest places of your heart. They'll bring 'Life' to those who find them, and healing to their whole body. Guard your heart above all else, for it determines the course of your life. You must decide in your own heart how much to give. And do not give reluctantly,, or in response to pressure. " I love a person who gives cheerfully." I'll generously supply all you need. You'll always have all you need and plenty left to share. As My Word says, "They share freely and give generously to the poor. Their good deeds will be remembered forever." Yes, you'll be enriched in every way so you can always be generous. And when you take your gifts to those who need them, they'll give thanks to Me. With two results, needs met and thankful hearts expressed joyfully before Me.

MY FATHER, I'll stay focused on You and I'll Listen for Your Words within my heart. You're a Continual God, ready always to express Your Amazing Love to me and to others through me. My heart is guarded, yet open to be a funnel of Your Light and Love to anyone You desire. I am Yours! Even now, I'll draw closer to You in this quiet place, to lean into You to receive deeply the wealth of all that enlightens my soul in Your Loving Presence. Lord, abundance is mine for the asking, when my motive is generous and pure. You gave me everything in Jesus, and I, in return want to give everything I have and everything I am, back to You in selfless abandon. I surrender all, Joyfully! In Jesus' Name, Amen!

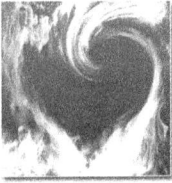

Psalm 23:1–6; Psalm 22:30–31

꧂

*I, your Lord, Am your Shepherd, you have all you need.
I let you rest in green meadows. I lead you beside peaceful
streams. I renew your strength. I guide you along the right
paths, bringing honor to My Name. Even when you walk
through the darkest valley, you'll not be afraid because I Am
close beside you. My rod and staff protect and comfort you.
I prepare a feast for you in the presence of your enemies.
I honor you by anointing your head with oil. Your cup
overflows with blessings. Surely My Goodness and unfailing
Love will pursue you all the days of your life, and you'll live
in My house forever. Oh My beloved, your children will also
serve Me. Yes, your future generations will hear about My
Signs and Wonders. My Righteous acts will be told to those
not yet born. They'll hear about everything I've done.*

MY LORD, my Shepherd, You supply all that I need. You're my Merciful Loving God. Your Peace is mine in Your Presence, and You're always with me. You never leave me, nor will You ever let me down. I can find You easily, if I look for You at any moment of time. I snuggle in close to You and lay my head on Your chest and breathe deep, the very Sound of Your Life-Giving Presence. You're both gentle and strong, full of continual Grace. You pre pare my day, and You lead me through it. I'll honor You in the day You've provided, because You've anointed me with the oil of Your Spirit to do so. You pursue me daily with gentle expressions of Your wondrous Ways, and I want to stay close by Your side, my King, forever. In Jesus' Name, Amen!

Matthew 19:14–15; Psalm 24:1–6, 8

*My beloved, "let the children come to Me. Don't stop them!
My Kingdom in Heaven belongs to those who are like
children." I place My Hand on their heads and bless them
before I leave. The earth is Mine, and everything in it. The
world and all of its people belong to Me. I laid the earth's
foundation on the seas, and built it on the ocean's depths.
Who can climb on My mountain? Who can 'Stand' in this
Holy place? Only those whose hands are clean and whose
hearts are pure, who do not worship idols and never tell lies.
They'll receive My blessing and have a right relationship
with Me, their Savior. Such people may seek Me, and
Worship in My Presence. Who Am I? The King of Glory!
Your Lord, 'Strong and Mighty!' Your Lord, 'Invincible in
Battle!'*

MY LORD, I belong to You! I'm in awe of Who You Are, yet I'm convinced
that I am Yours and You are mine! I come to You this day as a child, present-
ing myself in humility. My hands are clean, and my heart is pure before You
now. I've surrendered to You and I'll keep Your 'Light and Love' for others.
Everything in me knows that You're what we all need. Your Grace is sufficient and Your Peace is perfect! I'll not take my focus off of You, my King.
I receive Your blessing and I know an intimacy with You now, this day, like
never before. I Worship You, and in Your Presence I'm filled to overflowing
with Pure Joy! There's no one like You, my Savior. I'm in Love with You! In
Your Name my Jesus, Amen!

Matthew 20:25–28; Proverbs 6:6–8; Psalm 25:1–3

༄

My beloved, you know that the rulers in this world lord
it over their people, and officials flaunt their authority
over those under them. But, among you it is to be different.
Whoever wants to be a leader, must first be a servant, and
whoever wants to be first, must become your slave. Even My
Son, Jesus came not to be served, but to serve and to give
His Life as a ransom for many. Listen, take a lesson from
the ants, don't be lazy! Learn from their ways and become
wise! They have no prince, governor, or ruler to make them
work, but they labor hard all summer, gathering food for the
winter. I Am your Lord, give your life to Me. Trust in Me!
I'll not let you be disgraced, or let your enemies rejoice over
your defeat. No one who trusts in Me, will ever be disgraced;
disgrace comes to those who try to deceive.

LORD, the world is in much turmoil in these days, and yet it is obvious that
You are in the midst of it all. You're aware of all that the rulers of this world
are doing. You'll set in place leaders, and You'll remove them in Your time.
Trusting You is the thing I must do. You have us, all that are surrendered to
You, in the palm of Your Hand, and in the very center of Your will. We're in
Your clear view, we do not need to fear, not anyone but You! Serving others
is serving You, and this is what pleases You most. I'll not hold back when an
opportunity or assignment arises for me to be a radiant Light of Your Love to
someone. I say, 'Yes' Father, here I am Lord, Send me! You're my Shield, my
Comfort, and my King! And I'm Your Hands and Heart extended to the lost,
the dying, and the needy, every moment of every day! In Jesus' Name, Amen!

Matthew 16:24–25; Proverbs 5:1–2; Isaiah 59:17; Philippians 1:6

～

My beloved, if you want to be My follower, you must turn from selfishness, take up your cross, and follow Me. If you try to hang on to your life, you'll lose it. But if you give up your life for My sake, you'll save it. My Love, pay attention to My Wisdom; 'Listen carefully to My Counsel.' Then you'll show discernment, and your lips will express what you've learned. I've placed on you, My Righteousness as your Body Armor, and I placed the Helmet of Salvation on your head. I clothe you with a Robe of My Vengeance (Authority), and wrap you with a Cloak of My Divine, Passionate Love. Now be certain of this; I, your God, who began My transforming work in you, will surely continue until I've finally completed it, on the day when Jesus returns.

MY LORD, my God, I'll follow You all the days of my Life. I'll make sure that You alone are my focus, and nothing will hold me back from my intent on following You. I give up all of my Life, to serve You, closely paying attention to Your Wisdom and Truth. I'll speak the Truth You have placed within me whenever my heart discerns the need. I'll put on Your Armor daily, which includes Your Robe of Authority, coupled with Your Cloak of Love. And this will look just like my Jesus. I'm certain that You're at work within me, transforming me in the midst of the warfare and the righteousness that surround me. I'm secure that I'm safe in You, my God, and my Savior, forever. In Jesus' Name, Amen!

Acts 2:16–21, 25–26

❧

My beloved, as I stated through the prophet Joel; "In the Last days, I'll pour out My Spirit on all people. Your sons and daughters will prophesy. Your young men will see visions, and your old men will dream dreams. In those days, I'll pour out My Spirit even on My servants, men and women alike, and they'll prophesy. I'll cause wonders in the heavens above and signs on the earth below, blood, fire, and clouds of smoke. The sun will become dark, and the moon will turn blood red before the Great and Glorious day of My arrival! Everyone who calls on My Name, as Lord, will be saved." "You see that I, your Lord, am always with you. You'll not be shaken, for I Am right beside you. No wonder your heart is glad, and your tongue shouts out My Praises! Your body now rests in hope."

MY LORD, I sit in the stillness, resting in Your comforting Presence. I'm aware that the days ahead hold many things I don't know of yet. I'm not fearful because I know You are with Me, always. You pour out Your Spirit and Your Gifts of the Holy Spirit upon me. You give me prophetic dreams and visions to prepare me for the things that would be overwhelming. You present signs and wonders to build up my faith and to ready me for more intensity. When that Great and Glorious day arrives, I'll be Ready! Because You're My Lord, I'm Saved already. Nothing can shake me. You hold me in the palm of Your Hand. You call me the 'Apple of Your Eye' because You're watching me that closely. You are so close You're surrounding me. My spirit is at Peace, and I rest in You, Lord. My heart is Rejoicing in quiet Worship. In Jesus' Name, Amen!

Matthew 21:21–22; Psalm 127:1–2; Psalm 25:5–7

ꤱ

I tell you the truth, My beloved, if you have faith and don't doubt, you can do things that My Son Jesus did, and more! You can even speak to a mountain saying: "May you be lifted up and thrown into the sea," and it will happen. You can pray for anything, and if you have faith, you'll receive it. Remember, unless I, your Lord, build a house, the work of the builder is wasted. Unless I, protect a city, guarding it with armies will do no good. I lead you by My truth and teach you, for I'm your God and I save you. All day long put your hope in Me. Remember My compassion and unfailing Love, which I've shown you from long ago. I do not remember your rebellious sins from your youth. I remember you in the Light of My unfailing Love, for I Am Merciful.

LORD, I thank You for continually building up my faith. In the most amazing ways I see You actively displaying Your Greatness and my faith is strengthened. Your Presence is with me even when I'm unaware, yet I simply call out Your Name or whisper my need in a breath and immediately, in an instant I'm surrounded by You and secured. You give Your angels charge over me, and yet You ask me to walk in an attitude of authority, with boldness and Love. When I'm weak, You're Strong! I believe in You, and Your Love is unfailing. You mold me and make me on the inside and out, into the likeness of You. You teach me Your truths and You write Your Word on the inside of my heart. You don't remember my sins from long ago, so why should I? I think of You Lord, and I'm filled with Your Peace, Hope, and even Your Grace today. And I believe You! In Jesus' Name, Amen!

Psalm 26:3–8, 11–12; Titus 2:6–8

‿

My beloved child, you're always aware of My unfailing Love, and you've lived according to My Truth. Do not spend your time with liars, or hang out with hypocrites. Hate the gatherings of those who do evil, and refuse to join in with the wicked. Wash your hands to declare your innocence. Come to My Altar, singing songs of thanksgiving and testifying of My Wonders. Love My Sanctuary, it is the Place where My Glory dwells. You'll not be like that, You'll live your life with integrity. And I'll Redeem you and show you Mercy. You'll 'Stand' on solid ground and publicly Praise My Name! Encourage the young to live wisely. You, yourself must be an example to them by doing good works of every kind. Let everything you do reflect the integrity and seriousness of what you teach. Teach truth so that you won't be criticized. Then those who oppose you'll be ashamed and have nothing bad to say about us.

LORD, my God, I chose to live in the Light of Your Truth with integrity. I'll not be moved or drawn out by the lusts of the flesh, for I have completely surrendered my life to Your will and Your ways. I come to You today, to bow down, within the realm of Your Loving Presence. This is where I find the Peace that is rich and only dwells within Your Glory. You've Redeemed me, and I'll 'Stand!' For I'm secure in You, and I'll publicly express my Praise to You for all who will 'Listen!' I'll encourage the generations of Your Truth, and I'll Love them with integrity and excellence that comes from being in Your Will. I'll daily take time to be prepared before You, Intimately. And I'll serve You Lord, all of my days, trusting You to cause me to be a radiant, reflective expression of You. I Love You my Lord, and Savior. Because of You, I Love others also. Use me today I pray. In Jesus' Name, Amen!

Exodus 18:10–11; Exodus 19:5; Matthew 22:37–39; Psalm 27:7–8, 14

~

My beloved, Praise Me! I've rescued you from the Egyptians and from Pharaoh. I've rescued Israel from their powerful hand. You know I'm Greater than any god because I rescue My Own from the oppression of even the proud Egyptians. If you obey Me and keep My Covenant, you're My Own special treasure from among all the people of the earth for all the earth belongs to Me. You must Love Me with all your heart, soul, and mind. This is My first and greatest Commandment. The second is equally as important, 'Love your neighbor as yourself.' I hear you when you pray. I'm merciful and I do answer you. Your heart has heard Me say: 'Come and talk with Me.' And your heart responds: 'Lord I'm coming.' 'Wait patiently for Me, Be brave and courageous. Yes, wait patiently for Me.'

FATHER, I Praise You and Worship You for Your Amazing Ways. Your faithful Love endures through all generations. You protect and defend Your very Own. I'm blessed to be Yours. I know that there's no one like You. You created all and You're in all, nothing's impossible for You. I'll follow Your ways and stay near You, keeping watch on the path You've set before me. Trusting You, I'll hold tightly to Your Strong hand. I'll stay in Your Presence where there is no fear. I'll obey You, and Love others, too. Our intimate conversational relationship is the place I find wisdom and the courage to be brave in this life. I'll wait patiently in the quietness, for Your Sound, and for Your direction and truth for today! I wait! In Jesus' Name, Amen!

Proverbs 7:1–4; Acts 13:38–39

My Child, follow My advice, always treasure My commands. Obey My commands and Live! Guard My instructions just like you guard your own eyes. Tie them on your fingers as a reminder. Write them deep within your heart. Love wisdom like a sister, make insight a beloved member of the family. 'Listen, you're here to proclaim that through My Son, Jesus, there's forgiveness for sins. Everyone who believes in Him is declared right with Me. This is something the law of Moses could never do. I, your Lord, see you when you travel, and when you rest at home. I know everything you do. I know what you'll say before you say it. I go before you and follow you. I place My Hand of blessing on your head.

MY KING, as I come to our quiet sanctuary of Peace, where I'm surrounded by Your Presence, I find Wise counsel and understanding for my heart today. You're always with me, ready at any time to give me instructions in truth. You'll guide me always, and I'll follow Your lead. I'm aware of Your desires. I have many choices to make throughout my day. I'll always consider Your commands and Your Words, because they are in me, a part of my DNA. I'm being changed by You now. My insight is becoming pure, and as I go to share Your Love and forgiveness with others, watch over me Lord, in every way. Watch my words, my ways, and even my attitude. Let me know when I'm out of line, and correct me. Do not let me dishonor You in anyway. Keep Your Hand of blessing on me throughout this day. I need You! In Jesus' Name, Amen!

Matthew 24:4–14; Revelation 13:10b; Zechariah 4:6

My beloved, don't let anyone mislead you, for many will come in My Name, claiming 'I am the Messiah.' They'll deceive many. And you'll hear of wars and threats of wars, but don't panic. Yes, these things must take place, but the end won't follow immediately. Nation will go to war against nation, and kingdom against kingdom. There will be famines and earthquakes in many parts of the world. But all this is only the first of the birth pains, with more to come. Then you'll be arrested, persecuted, and killed. You'll be hated all over the world because you're My followers.' And many will turn away from Me and will betray and hurt each other. And many false Prophets will appear and will deceive many people. Sin will be rampant everywhere, and the love of many will grow cold. But, the one who endures to the end will be Saved. And the Good News about 'My Kingdom' will be preached throughout the whole world, so that all nations will hear it, and then the end will come. My people must endure persecution patiently, and stay faithful. Not by force, or by strength, but by 'My Spirit.' This is what I Say, your God, 'The Lord of Heaven's Armies!' I Am with you, even unto the end of the world.

MY LORD, my God, I ask You for Supernatural Wisdom and Strength to be alive and well within me, by Your Word. In times of troubles, problems, and pain, I do not want to run, but to 'Stand!' I want to 'Be Ready' for anything this world might bring. I'll walk in obedience to You because I know Your Voice! Your Steadfast Love is in me, and I'll grasp tight to Your Hand. I know that Your Spirit Lives in me and Your Word tells me that you'll never leave me or forsake me. I ask for the Courage to walk through every battle with Authority and Love! The Battle is Yours, I'll walk with You through it. When I see the signs of these times, I will not be afraid. Though my spirit grieves, I will not look back, but Press on! You are My Great Reward! Nothing compares to You! I'll walk by Faith and not by sight, knowing that the enemy is at work to destroy, I'll not be moved! You are my Staying Power and my Promise! You've Redeemed me by Your Blood and bought me with The Price. It Will all be Finished, and I know We Win! IN JESUS' NAME, Amen!

www.ingramcontent.com/pod-product-compliance
Lightning Source LLC
LaVergne TN
LVHW051252080426
835509LV00020B/2932